GW01018140

Published by R&A, The Netherlands.

Typeset with TEX, using the mkii version of the ConTeXt macro package.

ISBN 978-90-819840-5-8. Second Printing: ±90 small errors have been fixed.

Contact info: *info@enterprisechess.com*
Web site: *http://enterprisechess.com*
Suggested hashtag: *#eachess*

The world is not $\mathbb{Q}$, it is $\mathbb{R}$

*The most erroneous stories are those we think
we know best — and therefore never scrutinize
or question.*
Stephen Jay Gould

Contents

5

*In software, the chain isn't as strong as its
weakest link; it's as weak as all the weak links
multiplied together*
Steve McConnell — Code Complete

*Nothing is as dangerous in architecture as
dealing with separated problems*
Alvar Aalto

Prologue:
Loosely Coupled Spaghetti

SUPPOSE WE have a system for the approval of loans. The business logic has been put into a Business Rule Engine (BRE) system*. Our system has business rules and for a certain class of prospective customers, an extra check is needed (thus say the business rules). This check involves sending a message to a credit rating institute and waiting for the result. Our system will in those cases use our Enterprise Service Bus (ESB) to send a message to a server (which runs a service for this function, hence Service Oriented Architecture or SOA) which then handles the interaction with the credit rating institute via a dedicated secure link. Since we only do this check in a small percentage of cases, the server handling the requests and replies to the credit institute is limited in size and our secure link is narrow as well.

The system complies with all the current popular architectural terms, is up and running, and all is well.

---

* If you are not technical and terms like 'application server', 'caught exceptions', or 'web proxy' in the fragment that follows, do not immediately get you started, do not worry: there is no need to know what I am talking about here in a technical sense. You can read this without understanding any of the technical references. Just skip over them, their specifics are not important to the story. They are real enough, though. You can trust me on that, or ask your engineers.

Now, a credit crisis comes along. Suddenly, the credit risk of prospects becomes an important factor. "Simple", says the business consultant, "we just change our business rule so all but the 1% wealthiest of our prospects are checked against the records of the credit rating institute". It is a simple change to make, and thanks to our Business Rule Engine, no programmers are needed. Management sighs its relief. The change is made, the result is tested, and the whole new business rule goes into production…

…and immediately grinds to a halt because neither our server handling the interface to the credit ratings institute, nor the connection to the credit ratings institute are capable of handling this amount of activity. The program on our application server creates many 'time out' exceptions because the credit ratings institute does not reply fast enough, and as a result our application server dies from memory problems as it tries to handle all the loggings as a result of the caught exceptions in the application server. Because the application server has died, the web proxy server starts to present an incomprehensible error screen to the users, who en masse call the help desk. All these calls to the help desk forces the help desk people to put up a taped answer, frustrating the users even more, while the infrastructure engineers scramble to dig into the setup to find the root cause of the incomprehensible error screen on the web proxy server.

Now, people may say: this change should have been stress tested and of course it should have. But as both Dijkstra[1] and McConnel[2] have written: tests cannot prove the absence of errors. Besides, not all situations can be made so that actual real-world tests are possible.

This story, however, is not about how this problem should have been caught. This story is about the fact that we have created — with all our state of the art tooling, our ESB, our SOA and our BRE — a setup where you make a small change in one place and the setup starts to go massively wrong in another. Such a problem with interdependencies first appeared in computer programs during the sixties of the previous century, when programming was new and those programs started to become sizable (and thus complex) for the first time. The programs turned out to be very *brittle*; they broke easily. For the software architectural problem behind it, the phrase 'spaghetti code' caught on. Since our modern state of the art setup exhibits the same sort of behavior, we must conclude that we have spaghetti again. Loosely coupled spaghetti, but spaghetti nonetheless.

It is not that we cannot solve this particular example problem, or that it is a particular good example, it is that — with all our object orientation, service orientation and business rule abstractions — we are back in a situation where the word spaghetti applies again, roughly half a century after the term was first coined as a derogative term for something that should be avoided.

And not only do we still have spaghetti, even some old simplistic (and ineffective) remedies are still being practiced. If the application server can't handle it, your engineers will propose to 'solve' the problem by adding more computing power and memory to your servers. This 'solution', many of us will recognize, and as a result we all also have the experience that, while hardware is supposed to become cheaper all the time, technical infrastructure for large setups is still very expensive. But scaling up this hardware or that connection may (temporarily) 'solve' a particular problem, like the one from our example, but it is essentially the same kind of 'repair' as was undertaken fifty years ago when a programmer increased the size of some array in a computer program to prevent that program from crashing. Such a change may prevent the crash for now, but it does not address the root cause, and the problem generally crops up again and again until you fix the real reason why memory is filling up.

There was already talk of a 'software crisis' more than forty years ago[*]. And in 1986, Fred Brooks, famous author of *The Mythical Man-Month*[†] wrote[‡]:

> Of all the monsters who fill the nightmares of our folklore, none terrify more than werewolves, because they transform unexpectedly from the familiar into horrors. For these, one seeks bullets of silver that can magically lay them to rest.
>
> The familiar software project has something of this character (at least as seen by the non-technical manager), usually innocent and straightforward, but capable of becoming a monster of missed schedules, blown budgets, and flawed products. So we hear desperate cries for a silver bullet, something to make software costs drop as rapidly as computer hardware costs do.
>
> But, as we look to the horizon of a decade hence, we see no silver bullet. There is no single development, in either technology or management technique, which by itself promises even one order of magnitude improvement in productivity, in reliability, in simplicity.

---

[*] E.g. in Edsger Dijkstra's ACM Turing Award lecture in 1972 [Dij72].
[†] [Bro78]
[‡] [Bro87]. And I must say, I'm a bit envious. The man can write. This is beautiful prose, which I wish I could have written myself.

Brooks further argued that the (then) new methods (like object-orientation) had been able to minimize the (programmer-made) 'avoidable complexity'*, but that the 'essential complexity' could not be solved by clever methods, it was just a fact of the landscape. There was, as Brooks wrote, "no silver bullet".

The belief that problems, such as the one from our example, should be at least partly solvable has remained alive, even if, from the mid-nineties on, both the avoidable and the essential and irreducible complexities of the IT field have largely been the expected and accepted backdrop against which our trade is performed. Nobody talks about a software crisis anymore, if alone because staying in crisis mode is not feasible for decennium after decennium. Skilled IT or enterprise architects already know this and will not be surprised by the above example of 'spaghetti', it has become 'normal'. We are just not used to calling it 'spaghetti' anymore.

Now, the example above serves two objects. First, as a simple to understand warning for organizations and their non-technical managers, that there still is no silver bullet. The warning is not unimportant, as the industry is still rife with silver bullets for sale, all unknown when Brooks wrote his article. ESBs, BREs, SOAs, Agile, Scrum, Cloud computing, and all kind of platforms are often still sold as such (and believed in as such). For instance, while a bit on their return, Business Rule Engines have been popular with management, because they promise a shift from programmer to

---

* Brooks actually calls this 'accidental complexity', but 'avoidable' is better because this results not only from chance but more often from lack of skills.

the 'business consultant'[*], and thus away from the need of (incomprehensible, brittle and expensive) IT skills. Recent additions to the 'silver bullet' set are, for instance, Cloud, Agile, and Scrum. All worthwhile methods and technologies, certainly, but no silver bullets.

The fact is, that using an ESB, a BRE, SOA, Cloud, and all the others does not by itself provide stability, robustness, and good and future-proof systems. Without some of them, we might indeed end up with systems dying in a gridlock of hard dependencies, true, but the price we pay is an increase of loosely coupled spaghetti-like dependencies. And IT is not only complex, it is also fundamentally brittle because in itself, as a digital environment, it lacks the flexibility of human-type compensating behavior[†]. These days — thanks to networking and especially the internet — these dependencies range across all kinds of levels: software, application servers, networks and infrastructure, and even organizations. In part, it is managing this complexity of dependencies that the field of enterprise architecture was originally invented for.

---

[*] The current (2014) buzzword for this seems to be 'low code' development.
[†] This is even true if the software itself has been built with robustness in mind. Software may be robust under — for instance — bad data input, but that only means the software will not crash. It does not mean the software will still function as need be. At a business level, if software does not crash but also does not provide its intended service, the *business* will 'crash'. IT-centric ideas of robustness in fact ignore that it is the business that needs to be robust, and that requires more than just *technically stable* IT environments. It needs *functionally* stable IT environments, and that is something that digital technology fundamentally cannot deliver for reasons that are outside the scope of this book.

The consequence of problems like our 'loosely coupled spaghetti', and essential complexity in general, are the difficulty and high cost — in time and money, and in frustration — of *change** and *control*† in any organization that has a complex Business-IT landscape.

The issue at hand

Before computers were hooked up in all sorts of networks, writing good programs for them was already difficult, as illustrated by the quote from Brooks above. It was clear to many in the field that there were no silver bullets, and that better design — i.e. *system architecture* — was to be the solution.

When computers seriously started to get connected via networks, the problem became even more complex. System architecture alone was not enough, as there were many systems in play. The logical next design phrase was *enterprise architecture*. Thus a discipline was born.

Since then, networking has grown many orders of magnitude — from the small Local Area Networks, or LANs, of the eighties, via the narrow links of the initial internet and other Wide Area Networks (or WANs) of the nineties to the high speed broadband internet and the SaaS and Cloud solutions of today. During that period of rapid growth of connected systems, the discipline of enterprise architecture has been around as a way to fight the greatly increased complexities of the Business-IT world. And not just IT has become more

---

E.g. large IT projects.
E.g. risk and security.

complex, business has become more complex too, in a large part because IT enables it to become more complex.[3]. The complexity has grown in a close tango of Business and IT.

The question is: can enterprise architecture solve the problem of essential complexity or is it another silver bullet itself? Should enterprise architects maintain the position that the essential complexity is solvable at all? Because by maintaining that it is possible to solve the essential complexity probably, while not solving it at all, enterprise architects are positioning themselves constantly as amateurs and failures. And if complexity can be managed by enterprise architecture, how?

Sadly, we must conclude that enterprise architecture has not been a success story. True, the field is established, there are methods, frameworks, conferences, books, specialists, departments, and so forth, all very busy with enterprise architecture. But ask most organizations that do something with enterprise architecture, and you will not find many that are very satisfied with the *results*, even if they sometimes will say that they are satisfied with those that perform that function.

This book is an *argumentative* book. I will argue that much of the 'best practices' of the current enterprise architecture discipline have fundamental flaws, and that even performing them to perfection will not bring what they are supposed to bring.

First, I will roughly describe the essence of current practices, without going into detail of all the various frameworks and approaches. If you are acquainted with enterprise architecture, much of this will be familiar territory, so it might feel that I am taking too much time to get to the point.

There are however two important reasons for including this bit of ground work. First, this book is written for a wider audience; the reader should not need much prior knowledge. Second, we architects often differ subtly in our definitions and assumptions, so I need to share my framework of what enterprise architecture is, before discussing its flaws.[4]

Next, I will explain why our 'best practice' approaches most likely *cannot* work as expected, and also why we use them nonetheless. I'll draw on fundamental psychological, biological and philosophical subjects. But don't worry, I'll not go into these subjects very deep, even if these subjects do merit such attention. This is, by design, neither a heavy nor a complicated book.

My personal favorite philosopher, Ludwig Wittgenstein, by many seen as the most important analytic philosopher of the previous century, has once said that sometimes, looking at a tough philosophical question is like having entered a room without any other exit than the one you came in by. In such a situation, he argued, going to extreme lengths to try to answer the question is like trying to get out of that room without exits, except the door you entered the room by. You can always leave by that door of course, or in other words, you can leave the question for what it is, it is apparently not a question that can be sensibly answered. Enterprise architecture today is like someone who has entered that room and doesn't know that his approach is doomed. He needs to retrace his steps and go elsewhere. I will do that too. I will present a way out of the locked room, a way to get out of the corner enterprise architecture has painted itself in. Having tried that alternative approach over the last years have convinced me that it is possible, though not easy.

A personal note

This book grew out of my personal development as an enterprise architect. Before ending up as enterprise architect, I experienced many different roles in and around IT: software engineer and team leader for a large chemical company, software designer and IT infrastructure manager for an AI-related company, postmaster in the beginning years of the internet, a bit of sales, owner of my own small software development firm, civil servant working on government strategy for science & technology, manager of a department where a lot of high-tech research & development was going on, information strategist, and finally back to the more technical world of Business-IT, or enterprise, architecture.

When I returned to (enterprise) architecture I constantly felt unhappy about the state of affairs of that discipline. And I suspected that the remedies offered — often as 'best practice'[*] — were unlikely to work. They reminded me of the failed simple ideas that flourished at the start of the Cognitive Science/AI developments of the sixties and seventies of the previous century, that had been so eloquently unmasked by Hubert Dreyfus in his wonderful book *What Computers Can't Do*[†].

My own ideas on how it *might* work slowly matured. When I had the chance to implement these ideas, the vague ideas met their first clash with reality[‡]. They turned out to work, but I also experienced the problems and bottlenecks of

---

[*] One of the most to be distrusted phrases in our industry.

[†] [Dre92]

[‡] Speaking of which, in case you are curious: the statement on the opening page is explained in the endnotes appendix[5].

trying to do that — and I experienced the necessary failures to sharpen my understanding.

Somewhere during that period, when I was trying to explain in a positive manner (instead of critiquing the basic problems with existing enterprise architecture approaches) to my environment what my ideas were about and how they differed from 'best practice', I thought of the basic analogy of enterprise architecture and playing chess. I have been using that analogy very effectively since, to explain enterprise architecture, why it fails so often, why many of its standard assumptions are misguided, and how I think it should be executed.

As mentioned above, this is by design not a heavy volume, and I have severely limited references to everything ever written about enterprise architecture that I know of[*]. It is small, because — besides addressing my peers — I also want non-architects such as general management to understand *why* fighting complexity and unpredictability is so difficult, and *what* can be done about it. A bit of practical information[†] that may be useful if you want to practice enterprise architecture along the lines of the ideas in this book has been relegated to the appendices, so it will not get in the way of a quick read but are available when required.

I would like to thank Guido van Kilsdonk, Joost Melsen, Jean-Baptiste Sarrodie, and Wil Scheijvens for the feedback received on various drafts of this book. I also want to thank

[*] For instance, you will not find a reference to the TOGAF, FEAF, DYA, or other enterprise architecture frameworks in the Bibliography, even though they are mentioned here and there in a sideline — this is *not* a book about (existing) enterprise architecture frameworks.
[†] Background information, templates, ...

Joost Melsen specifically for valuable discussions during the last couple of years — when the ideas now written down in this book were put into practice. His critical remarks on my rough ideas made those ideas substantially better, and his exceptional qualities as an enterprise architect were indispensable. He is the best enterprise architect I know.

I am also indebted to a couple of authors. A few of the most important ones for me are philosophers: Ludwig Wittgenstein, P.M.S. Hacker and Hubert Dreyfus. Let nobody tell you that analytic philosophy has no practical value; the sort that is closely related to the real world is. I also would like to mention the editors of the *New Scientist* magazine for creating an excellent gateway to the wider world of science & technology*.

I would like to apologize to Renée, Renske and Mark Douwe for what they had to suffer while I was writing this (and during the years I was — sometimes painfully — being taught by exposure of my ideas to the real world).

Finally, I'd like to thank you for purchasing and reading this little book. I trust you will enjoy it. If you want to discuss it with me, use the email address *info@enterprisechess.com*. More discussion and articles may appear on the book's web site: *http://enterprisechess.com*. On Twitter, I suggest using the hashtag *#eachess*.

Heerlen, December 2014,
Gerben Wierda

---

* And no, I'm not trying to kiss their most illustrious bottoms.

*If you think good architecture is expensive, try
bad architecture*
Brian Foote and Joseph Yoder

1   An Inconvenient Truth

IN THE HALF century or so that human kind has had IT, the IT sector has increasingly wrestled with the fact that IT projects often fail in one way or another. As Dijkstra once observed[*]:

> As long as there were no machines, programming was no problem at all; when we had a few weak computers, programming became a mild problem, and now that we have gigantic computers, programming has become a gigantic problem. In this sense the electronic industry has not solved a single problem, it has only created them, it has created the problem of using its products[†]. To put it in another way: as the power of available machines grew by a factor of more than a thousand, society's ambition to apply these new machines grew in proportion, and it was the poor programmer who found his job in this exploded field of tension between the ends and the means. The increased power of the hardware, together with the perhaps more dramatic increase in its reliability, made solutions feasible that the programmer had not dared to dream about a few years before. And now, a few years later, he had to dream about them and even worse, he had to transform such dreams into reality! It is no wonder that we found ourselves in a software crisis.

As Dijkstra's 'gigantic computers' are pretty puny compared to those of today, and as our computers have since

---

Edsger Dijkstra — *The Humble Programmer* [Dij72]
[GW:] Such as the ESBs, BREs, etc., mentioned in the prologue.

become massively connected, it is no wonder that these problems are known to many in our field. And it takes only a few large unsuccessful IT projects to make it clear to everybody involved that something is amiss. For example, a large Dutch government agency* ran a large IT project from around 1998 until 2013. I estimated that at the time I stopped watching, the total cost up until then had been M€100 and effectively the money was completely wasted. The responsible parties, though, played hide and seek† for five more years and finally in 2013 the agency admitted the project had failed and according to their estimates it had cost M€100. My personal estimate is that is has cost at least 50% more than that. I'm not singling these people out, there are far too many of these examples around.[7]

In 1994, the Standish Group published a famous report based on surveys from the industry that concluded that 31% of IT projects failed outright: money spent and nothing to show for it. This report shocked the IT world and put the 'Software Crisis' to the front page of our IT consciousness. There have been many rightful criticisms of the Standish approach, both in terms of selection of parties to survey and their methodology[8], but everybody does agree that running

---

* I do not want to single them out, so I have anonymized this.

† Reliable reporting on large software disasters is almost nonexistent. In this case, an architecture audit conducted by the project's own new architect, two external professionals and a fourth one from a neighboring agency, reported in 2007 that the project's results were unusable to the extent that 'repairing' would equate to 'rebuilding' (or in other words 'broken beyond repair'). This was later reported to parliament as that the project could be 'repaired'. The parliament, generally an institute that lacks IT know how, never found out that they had effectively been lied to.[6]

large IT projects is difficult and expensive and the projects fail (or fail in part) more often than is acceptable. Those in the projects suffer too. Steve McConnell, paraphrasing Thomas Hobbes, observed: "Life on a poorly run software project is solitary, poor, nasty, brutish, and hardly ever short enough."*.

While the complexity problem has grown with the increase in power and connectivity of computing technology, so have development methods changed over the years. There are three major area's which have been improving.

The first has been technology: better methods for software development have been created, starting with 'Structured Programming' of the sixties until (for instance) 'Object-Orientation' of the eighties and beyond. Object-orientation has been scaled to the system level to get Service Oriented Architectures (SOA) and so forth. With new technological ideas, the tooling to support these ideas improved as well: from better programming languages until better tools to support the developer. And this innovation has been ongoing to this day.

But pretty soon it was found that better development technology alone was not enough to prevent failure. For one, developers had to produce results that catered to the wishes of the users. And developers experienced that users were often vague about and (what was worse) volatile in their demands during development, as if — while building a bridge across a river — halfway there came a requirement not to hinder shipping at all, not even temporary, which turned the bridge project overnight into a tunnel project. When a

[McC04]

project failed (or started to fail) developers generally directed blame at the users, with their vague and above all volatile demands.

This led to the second type of project improvements: improved requirements management, and improved design efforts. Clearly, a project needed to control its environment if there was to be the stability needed for success. The first methods were strongly top-down. They started with requirements, which were translated to functional (behavioral) design, which were translated to technical designs which were translated to actual software. The nickname for these kinds of methods is 'waterfall'. Sometimes 'waterfall' worked, but more often it did not, and the term has since become a derogatory term in IT, even if it is in reality still practiced in a large majority of projects.

The requirements remained vague and volatile for most projects (by definition, since the projects were about support for real-world, mostly human, processes) and in waterfall methods this means that at each clarification or change, one is supposed to go back to the top of the waterfall to rework the entire project top-down. In reality this never happens and the end result is generally that the software changes to cater to the changed requirements and the upstream materials (technical designs, functional designs, architecture documents) are never adapted and become obsolete, thus, guidance for development erodes. Waterfall may have worked here and there, but improvements to the success rate of projects remained scarce.

And if only the users were to blame, life would be simple. But more often than not, the volatility came from elsewhere. A regulator or law-maker changing business rules for the company, increasing awareness about security, sudden reorganizations, new business opportunities, a disruptive new competitor, new tooling, the list is endless. And not only is the list unknowable (because it is endless), it is also unpredictable. It is impossible to predict what changes are coming from what direction. This is a key problem for most classic project management approaches in IT projects: these approaches try to deliver limited and predictable — and because we are dealing with digital computers: strictly logical — results in environments which are not logical but vague and contradictory, and most of the time unknowable and unpredictable. Worse even: many unpredictable changes come from within the project's direct environment of which everybody silently assumes it can be in control: other projects of the same organization, changed or additional organizational goals, et cetera. Most IT projects are executed within a world which is best characterized by 'partly chaotic'. Classic 'certainty building'-oriented project management is only partly able to fight that, and its remedies are not always palatable to the organization. A good project manager is supposed to religiously guard his scope and be strong in the face of all kinds of pressure to change, but the approach cannot always work: you just cannot always ignore the environment or place it out of scope.[*]

In reaction to the chaotic nature of the environment, early inflexible project management methods have evolved into the modern, more 'agile', methods of today, e.g. a very

_____

[*] And even if you are allowed to place a subject out of scope, a result is most likely a glaring hole in your landscape. Project successful, landscape damaged.

good method like PRINCE2, where you start with a good business case and then organize your project to handle *change*, continuously guarding the business case. The best project management methods and the best project managers do not fight change, they *handle* (manage) it, but based on a different 'invariant' than scope: the business case[*].

The difficulties of 'waterfall' have also led to a recent counter movement with more adaptive and less formal approaches to IT development itself, often grouped under the generic 'agile' umbrella. These are less new than it seems. Adaptive development methods are almost as old as more formal methods. For instance, 'rapid prototyping' was a buzzword for adaptive methodology in the nineties. Agile, therefore, looks a bit like another 'silver bullet' of todays IT development practices. Just as with waterfall methods, there is worth and truth in the current silver bullets, but they also have a lot of pitfalls. For agile, for instance, these include that it does not scale very well, can be very inefficient, et cetera[†].

Even with agile methods available, most project managers today try to *oppose* change to the project and strictly guard its scope, an attitude that sometimes is a solution that is worse than the problem, because it limits intelligent handling of

---

[*] An interesting contrast to 'waterfall' and a lesson to be learned for IT.

[†] In the worst case, 'agile' as a term is used as an argument against any sort of architectural process. In that case, the architectural approach is seen as blocking good progress and the often heard quote is 'just let it happen', and 'we take the evolutionary approach'. But unless our enterprises can be as wasteful as evolution often is in nature (death and extinction are essential and accepted, and *what* survives, what the outcome is, is irrelevant), conscious design will remain the norm for human engineering.

inevitable change. It has become clear that project and requirements management do not solve the problem and 'architecture' has emerged as a third instrument to handle the complexities of real life IT projects. You need not only manage the requirements and planning of the solutions, you need also to manage the content of the solutions itself.

The massive problems we experience when trying to run IT projects in a way that is predictably successful is a fact that is both inconvenient and true, but not so much 'an inconvenient truth' in the sense that it is a truth we rather would sweep under the rug. We all are more or less aware of these problems and they have become accepted backdrop we tend to live with as best as we can. The 'inconvenient truth' of this chapter's title is another one.

The truth we must face

So, after having experienced that requirements management, strict project controls, waterfall design, methods such as rapid prototyping, and all the hyped-up silver bullets did not have a large effect on the ever problematic large IT projects and complex landscapes, the IT world turned to the idea of 'architecture' as a means to get the interdependencies and the uncertainty in future direction under control. Instead of a haphazard collection of projects, each with its own (vague) ideas about the development of solutions for the enterprise, there should be an overall view on what is required so that projects are of a good quality and are *aligned with all business* interests and the business' environment, not just the particular business goal they have been called into existence for, and *aligned with each other*. The problem was initially seen to be 'alignment' of various sorts and the solution was *Enterprise Architecture*, though it was not initially called that way.

Various Enterprise Architecture methodologies have arisen to manage/produce this alignment. With names like Zachman, DYA, DoDAF, MODAF, TOGAF, IAF, FEAF, NAF, NORA, ESAAF, GEA, TEAF, LEAD, AGATE, Praxeme, TRAK, Dragon1, SABSA*, they now are an integral part of large IT-oriented change management.

Enterprise Architecture is generally seen to be about envisioning an enterprise-wide 'future state' you want to work towards. Such a future state is not just some sort of planned landscape, it generally also consists of guidelines and principles that guide the evolution towards that landscape. Such a future state and such guidelines are supposed to bring focus to a myriad of change initiatives and has to make sure that projects (a) are coherent and (b) work towards a common (and desirable) goal. Often, we are confronted with pictures of the current state landscape and pictures of a future state landscape. Between those two, we can construct via gap-analysis the changes we need to effectuate to go from the (often problematic) 'now' to the (ideal) future. It is logical and seems to make sense.

Now, here is our very inconvenient truth: *Enterprise Architecture as a discipline has so far largely failed to produce the intended results.*

---

* Security architecture framework.

This is reflected in many ways. The most important one is of course that the same sort of chaos that enterprise architecture is meant to prevent still exists everywhere, regardless of the fact that we now have had the concept of enterprise architecture for approximately thirty years. Something is clearly not working, or everybody would have adapted the successful approaches by now. Another clear sign is that enterprise architecture functions or departments are reorganized on a regular basis, far more often in my observations than other (established) specialized functions such as Legal, HR, Facilities, et cetera. I have seen at one organization that, within six years, the central enterprise architecture function was reorganized four(!) times. Now, an organization does not go through all that reorganization trouble if it is satisfied with what it has. So, it clearly isn't. And this pattern is seen everywhere.

There are many reasons why organizations are dissatisfied with enterprise architecture. Of course they are largely dissatisfied because of the very limited effectiveness, the end-result so to speak. But even while the hopes are still up that enterprise architecture *should* work, organizations also seldom like what they experience on a day to day basis when working with enterprise architecture departments. Part of this is unavoidable as enterprise architecture is meant to limit the total freedom the organization has in changing itself. Such a limitation naturally breeds resistance and dissatisfaction. But there is more wrong than just that.

For instance, enterprise architecture functions are often ineffective 'high-over' activities of which many people in the organization feel that the work they do does hardly relate to the practical reality people are in. On the other hand, if the enterprise architects do effectively interfere with reality, they tend to be seen as an impractical bottleneck/'stonewalling change' type of function. Their abstract pictures are too far above the needs of the day, their principles and guidelines are idealistic and impractical, and to be circumvented or ignored during actual work, and they are often liked best when they stay out of the way. Which is a rather surprising situation for a discipline that is supposed to be the one that gets us out of the mess everybody hates, a discipline that should be somewhat mature after thirty years of existence.

Another clear sign is the lack of true success stories at (enterprise architecture) conferences and in the literature. Enterprise architecture conferences are never about real enterprise architectures in whatever form. They are generally about enterprise architecture frameworks, tools and techniques. They are about how to get the organization to listen (a subject that signals that the organizations clearly do not listen at all). The conferences consist of people active in the field talking about methodology that *should* work but that has never been *proven to* work. E.g. speakers may talk about how useful principles are, but practical examples of principles are seldom mentioned and proof that using principles really works is never presented. It is as if the enterprise architecture world is a world separate from the real world of organizations, some sort of abstraction of it. Of course, any field needs its own internal discussions on methods and techniques, but enterprise architecture seems a field of nothing *but* methodology and techniques. When is the last time you heard a story of a CEO that his company

31

was successful or saved because all the brilliant work done in enterprise architecture?*

So, let's face our own inconvenient truth: enterprise architecture doesn't really work the way we have assumed for thirty years it would.

---

* This statement is unfair, I know. The same is true for HR, legal and many other disciplines. And what management generally reports (or implies) is that success is the success of *management*†. Still, as far as I have observed, while HR or legal and the others are sometimes mentioned, enterprise architecture is not mentioned at all.

And frankly they are right. If enterprise architecture functions, this is a result of proper management, not so much of the enterprise architects who are just 'tools' in that effort.

The ultimate goal of the architect [. . .] is to create a paradise. Every [. . .] product of architecture [. . .] should be a fruit of our endeavour to build an earthly paradise for people
Alvar Aalto

2 Why Enterprise Architecture?

BEFORE WE dig into the question why enterprise architecture is not a success, not even after thirty years, we should look closely at the goals enterprise architecture is meant to support or attain. And that brings us back to the observation from Edsger Dijkstra in the previous chapter: when there were no computers, creating IT solutions was no problem, when we had a few weak computers it became a mild problem and now that we have extremely powerful computers[*] it has become a gigantic problem. And these days, we not only have extremely powerful computers, we have a gigantic network of them in a sort of loosely coupled spaghetti[†]. It is no wonder the enterprise architecture field started in the eighties of the previous century, as it was the time that computers for the first time started to be connected in networks in a serious way, thus creating the 'enterprise architecture' subject on top of the 'system architecture' subject that was already on the mind of most IT professionals.

Compared with the time of Dijkstra's observation (1972), and now (2014), computing power has multiplied with a factor of something like 150,000,000, assuming the number of computers grows by a factor of three every ten years[*▶] and

---

And what is worse: they will continuously become more powerful for years to come.
And what is worse: the number of networked computing devices will grow swiftly for years to come.

using some sort of Moore's Law for the power per computer[*]. Incidentally, this might be one of the reasons enterprise architecture has been unable to cope: over the last three decennia, its methods had to contend with a problem that became three hundred thousand times as large[†]. Actually, with the increase of many complexities, it is really impressive that we are still able to build and implement large working IT systems at all. We are definitely not only doing things wrong, we are also doing things right.

Who needs EA anyway?

Back to the original question: what problems is enterprise architecture supposed to address? Well, first we may ask ourselves: who, actually, has a *need* for enterprise architecture? Well, obviously not that shoe repair shop in the mall. It does have an enterprise architecture, but its IT might be limited to a single computer running the cash register and accounting.

[*◄] We seem to be on the threshold of another large increase of connected computers. More and more physical devices become computerized — the Internet of Things (IoT) — and we might see a massive increase in connected devices in the coming years.[9]

[*] This astronomical[10] growth is so much 'there' that we tend to ignore it.

[†] This is a completely exaggerated guess with many factors not taken into account. For instance, on the one hand, we established all sorts of levels of abstraction, such as ESBs, SOA, Object-Orientation that limit the transfer of complexity to higher levels. But on the other hand, complexity might increase as an exponent instead of as a factor of connectedness, in which the situation is a lot worse. All in all, we might safely assume that the enterprise architecture problem has grown in step with the growth in the number of (networked) computers, roughly an order of magnitude in the thirty years that enterprise architecture has existed.

There is no need to make a lot of fuss about that setup. A 500-FTE* factory that turns out those enormous propelling screws for large ships also doesn't need it. They may not have more than twenty to thirty people who use IT for sales, marketing, accounting and so forth. Again, not a setup that is difficult to manage for one or two IT engineers. But an asset manager that manages hundreds of billions of euros in assets has a hideously complex landscape of processes and IT systems, even if it had roughly the same number of employees as the aforementioned screw-producing factory. Clearly, the need for enterprise architecture is a function of the complexity of the Business-IT landscape.

So, given that enterprise architecture is about managing complexity, what is it going to bring us? Well, there are roughly three reasons why we want to engage in enterprise architecture:

- *To prevent IT-chaos* in medium and large landscapes. Preventing chaos is required for our Business-IT landscape to be robust, flexible and cost-effective, which are the ultimate goals. For this, we also need to get (IT-)change under control so it does not autonomously produce that chaos.

  This is the main and original goal of enterprise architecture. This is why it was invented in the first place. These days, you'll see a lot of attention to strategy, business architecture, and all that, but what should not be forgotten is that a main and major goal

---

Full Time Equivalent, the number of workers in terms of full jobs.

remains preventing chaos to ensue from the continuous change of the Business-IT landscape.

- **To make sure the Business-IT landscape fits the strategic business goals.** This has often been labelled 'Business–IT alignment'. It is about making sure that the IT landscape we have in a few years time fits the goals we have as a business. If our goal is to transform ourselves from a Business-to-Business (B2B) to a Business-to-consumer (B2C) company, for instance, we should make sure that we get the IT to support that different kind of customer, e.g. web shops and such, but also different processes, different kinds of roles for our employees, et cetera.
- **To make sure the Business profits from opportunities enabled by IT.** On the one hand we want an IT landscape that fits our business. But another nice thing is to be able to change our business based on opportunities provided by IT innovations. If your whole architecture is based on 'batch production' of information, adapting to a world where customers, using mobile platforms, expect interaction and direct manipulation is rather problematic. Alignment as well, but in the other direction: 'IT-Business alignment'.

As you can see, all three have something to do with change. The first is a quality aspect of change: we want change to produce a quality landscape and not chaos. The other two are about how IT change follows business change or the other way around.

These three goals are presented somewhat in order of maturity. The first thing you need to do is prevent chaos from emerging. If you have that, you are able to change your IT landscape according to your strategic business requirements and if you are really mature, you are in a situation that new IT innovations can be easily incorporated in your business and your business has become 'agile' in reacting to that IT innovation. The three goals may also be seen as being presented in order of 'required for agility'[*]. In fact, we could characterize the three reasons in order of agility/maturity as:

- We need structure[†] in our landscape;
- We want our structure to *follow* strategy;
- We want our structure to *enable* strategy.

This order of maturity/agility is one of the reasons enterprise architecture is often experienced as conservative. Some enterprise architects know that Business-IT alignment in either direction is difficult to attain if your landscape is a chaotic mess. Hence, they may initially be focused on getting order in the chaos as a prerequisite. Such enterprise architects are experienced as opposed to change. Other architects may focus on the Business–IT alignment initially, embracing change. But if they do not take care of the chaos, there is no fertile ground for fundamental change and their seeds fall on infertile ground.

Though 'agile' fans may argue that given the chaos, agile methods can cope better as change initiatives discover the problems 'on the go', so instead of trying to prevent chaos, one could employ change methods that are more robust under chaos. There is of course a bit of truth in that, but we are now discussing the goals of enterprise architecture, not the goals of agile development methods.

Of IT, in other words: architecture

It's all about *change*

Given that it is all about change, we might phrase the problems that enterprise architecture is meant to solve on a day-to-day basis as:

- In change initiatives, choices are being made that are not in line with the company's **future, unknown** requirements. Above all, projects deal with *current* requirements.
- In change initiatives, choices are being made in different parts of the organization that conflict with each other (de facto not in line with **current, unmanaged** requirements)
- In change initiatives, choices are being made that are suboptimal, e.g. bad for continuity, cost (maintenance, change), timeliness, flexibility, etc. (de facto not in line with **current, unmanaged** requirements)

Essential 'types' of the requirements that come from the goals are highlighted here. At first sight, the last two seem manageable, as they are about requirements we can know. We just must learn to manage them effectively. In practice, though, given the complexity (interdependency and so forth), these are already pretty daunting. But the first one looks completely impossible: how on earth can we take *unknown* requirements into account? Still, it is a (not always explicitly stated) major goal of enterprise architecture. Let's see in the next chapter how generally enterprise architecture approaches try to solve these problems and attain their goals.

Architecture has curled up in a ball and it's about itself. It has found itself either as a freakshow, where you're not sure if it's good or bad but at least it's interesting, or at the behest of forces of commerce
David Chipperfield

No architecture is so haughty as that which is simple
John Ruskin

3 The Orthodoxy

ET US RETURN to the problems enterprise architecture has to solve, as described on page 38, but stressing a different aspect of those problems:

- In change initiatives, ***choices*** are being made that are not in line with the company's future, unknown requirements (projects deal with current requirements)
- In change initiatives, ***choices*** are being made in different parts of the organization that conflict with each other (de facto not in line with current, unmanaged requirements)
- In change initiatives, ***choices*** are being made that are suboptimal, e.g. bad for continuity, cost (maintenance, change), timeliness, flexibility, etc. (de facto not in line with current, unmanaged requirements)

What all these problems have in common is that it is all about the *choices* we make every day when we change our business-IT landscapes. What kind of choices are we talking about? Well, practical ones, such as:

- We need to create reports for our clients and the regulator. Do we source the reports from the accounting system, from the data warehouse or both? Choosing the accounting system saves us a step (because we don't have to copy the accounting data over to the data warehouse before we can report), but requires us to add extra data, such as benchmark data) to the accounting system because it is needed to create the reports (and not for the accounting process).

- We are selecting a new risk management system. Which one do we take? That the new system conforms to all our must-have business requirements is of course the main point. But if you buy a system, you are also buying a part of your architecture: how does the system integrate with other systems? How does data get in and out? What infrastructure is needed to run the system?[*]

- Which means do we use when we integrate platforms? How are automated processes scheduled? Do we use an Enterprise Service Bus? And if so, which functions should it perform and which functions should be left to the other systems?

- We need to replace both our accounting and our data warehouse system. If we do accounting first, we get an intermediate landscape[†] where we have to connect the new accounting system to the old data warehouse. If we do the data warehouse system first, we have to connect the new data warehouse to the old accounting system. Both are landscapes that are temporary. Which order (which intermediate architecture) is best?

---

[*] Buying a system or platform is buying *canned architecture*, something you have limited control over; an aspect that is often forgotten in the selection process. This is also true for the cloud, cloud-based solution have an architecture that becomes part of our organization's Business-IT landscape when we integrate their use in our business. See appendix A for more on cloud architecture.

[†] Or in enterprise architecture speak: a 'plateau'.

These are examples of 'large' choices. But there are also many small choices, made every day, that change the landscape.

Enterprise architecture is about ensuring that these choices are made sensibly from the perspective of our goals: no chaos, Business–IT alignment and IT–Business alignment. An enterprise architecture setup that is not able to influence exactly those choices could as well not be there. So, how has the enterprise architecture discipline generally been set up to influence those choices and to reach those objectives? What is the 'best practice'?

First, enterprise architecture as a business function has always been a *central* function. This is logical: after all it is about the organization as a whole, about its future and about its coherence. You need the central perspective to address these issues. The question then becomes: how should a central department ensure that all the different change initiatives do not produce chaos?

The classic enterprise architecture setup

Classically, the central enterprise architecture functions have tried to reach these goals using the following means:

- Define a 'future state architecture' (FSA), a not too-detailed future landscape* that the organization works towards. Often, some attention is paid to the 'current state architecture' (CSA)[11], at the same low level of detail as the FSA so that a gap-analysis can be made.

In Dutch, this is often called 'de stip op de horizon' (the spot on the horizon).

Such a gap-analysis is intended to feed portfolio management, from the gap between CSA and FSA follows which projects the organization must execute to get to its wished-for future state.*

- Define principles and guidelines for the change initiatives. Architectural principles and guidelines are meant to set limitations on the freedom of change initiatives so that there is less freedom to create the chaos that ensues if change initiatives are left to their own devices. In some setups, the use of guidelines is extended to a sort of 'building permit system'. Change initiatives propose a design (that is supposed to follow the guidelines and principles) and a check is performed by the enterprise architecture function and if the enterprise architecture function agrees it hands out a 'permit'. This last, very formalized, approach is not often practiced, though.

---

* Future state architecture is sometimes called the SOLL-architecture (from the German word for 'must' or 'should') and the current state is then likewise called the IST-architecture (from the German word for 'is'). I will therefore use the term IST-Gap-SOLL for this aspect of the classical enterprise architecture setup.

TheFEA (Federal Enterprise Architecture Framework) of the US government calls these 'baseline' and 'target' architectures.

Gartner's Enterprise Architecture framework, too, is based on a process that starts with identifying where the organization is going, basing a desired setup on that and then trying to move towards that setup.

The ANSI/IEEE Std 1471-2000 standard, which is most often quoted*, reflects this idea of enterprise architecture. It defines architecture as:

> The fundamental organization of a system, embodied in its components, their relationships to each other and the environment, and the principles governing its design and evolution.

Some methodologies start with the future state and then define the principles and guidelines. Some start with principles and guidelines and then define the future state. Some do this concurrently.[13]

The basic structure of the classical setup of enterprise architecture in organizations is shown in figure 3.1:

In that figure, 'EA=Central' stands for the organization's (central) enterprise architecture function. To ensure that change initiatives are aligned with the goals of enterprise architecture, it produces a future state, principles and guidelines and (potentially) 'building permits'. In the figure, what is being influenced by enterprise architecture is in this book called a 'domain'. A 'domain' can be many things. A domain can be a project, or a business unit, or a department. In fact, everything that has or changes a 'Business-IT landscape' is called a 'domain' here. So, this figure covers both enterprise architecture governing the design in projects as well as the changes in architectures of business units. The players are different, the pattern is the same. These domains engage in 'solution architecture'*▸, that is, the design choices made in

---

Still more often than the slightly different and most recent (2011) version ISO/IEC/IEEE 42010. That one says: "fundamental concepts or properties of a system in its environment embodied in its elements, relationships, and in the principles of its design and evolution".[12]

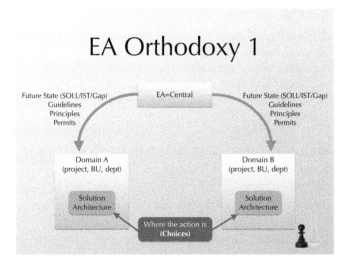

Figure 3.1 The classic enterprise architecture setup

change initiatives. Those 'solution architectures' are what 'enterprise architecture' is to influence if it is to make an impact. And for that it uses the Future State Architecture and the principles and guidelines.

There are, however, a couple of problems with this industry-standard 'best practice' approach.

---

*◄ The field of enterprise and IT architecture is not very precise in its definitions. The term 'solution architecture' is sometimes used for the architecture of a particular tool or platform. I sometimes use the term 'change architecture', but that too has different uses, so in this book I use the term 'solution architecture' for an architecture of a solution (for a business problem or wish).

The trouble with IST-Gap-SOLL*

The IST-Gap-SOLL approach is obvious from a goal-oriented point of view. And goal-orientation is something that comes naturally to both people and organizations.[†] But in practice, a concrete goal works only in a few limited enterprise architecture situations, and there are a couple of reasons for that.

The first reason is that if you want to direct change initiatives that themselves may be sizable and take a non-trivial amount of time (years, often), you need to make a SOLL-architecture that lies maybe four or five years in the future, maybe even further away as large changes in complex organizations may take years — and you can't do them all concurrently. In a period of that duration, the situation of the organization changes in so many ways that the SOLL-architecture becomes obsolete long before it is even remotely attained. IST-Gap-SOLL also suffers from the same problem as the 'waterfall' software engineering methods: if the assumptions of the whole plan change, either because of external influences or because of strategic changes, the envisioned target state has become invalid and it cannot be used to direct change initiatives anymore. It might even obstruct

---

[*] See footnote on page 44.

[†] In fact, this approach sees the overall enterprise architecture as if it is a kind of 'super-project' with a clear goal. While enterprise architects will time and again try to explain to the organization that enterprise architecture is not a 'product' or a 'project' or a 'project result', but that it is a (continuous) *process*, they ruin it immediately by setting it up along classic project-based goal-oriented lines like this.

them. In other words: IST-Gap-SOLL fits the volatility of real organizations* not very well.

There is another problem. A picture of 'heaven on earth, five years from now' necessarily lacks detail. But in the end, those details are what influences the emergence of chaos in the first place. A nicely defined high level SOLL-architecture therefore lacks the *relevant* details that make it a reliable way to fight a core problem enterprise architecture has to solve: emerging chaos. It is largely meant to aid the goal of Business–IT alignment, but as stated earlier, trying to create alignment — of the Business–IT or IT–Business variant — on top of a de facto chaos has little chance of success.

Enterprise architects know this of course. Which is why their approach is generally two-pronged. By and large, alignment is the intended result of the IST-Gap-SOLL approach, chaos is to be prevented with principles, guidelines and potentially 'building permits'.

Comply and (subsequently) die

Somewhere during the last decennium of the previous millennium, I visited the enterprise architecture outfit of a large bank. I do not recall exactly the reason of the visit, but I recall clearly that we ended in the room of the enterprise architects with a couple of desks and some computers on them. Also in that room was a shelf. And on that shelf stood

---

* This is especially true for organizations that are complex enough to require enterprise architecture in the first place. In general, the more an organization requires the benefits of enterprise architecture, the more volatile its 'extended context' is and the less IST-Gap-SOLL works. A real Catch-22.

something like twenty large binders, some 1.5 to 2 meters in shelf space altogether. Those binders contained this banks's *reference architecture*, which almost exclusively consisted of principles, guidelines and other comparable items (policies, suggestions, explanations, examples and so forth). What had started as an initiative to write up the principles and guidelines that would guide development in the bank and prevent the chaos, had grown and grown, with new exceptions, extra cases, new rules, et cetera. When I visited them, they were still very proud of their accomplishment. And indeed, from the perspective of work being put into it, it was a huge accomplishment.

Many organizations (including governments) during that period went through such a phase in enterprise architecture. They all ended up with huge, so-called, 'reference' architectures with uncounted rules and regulations. There was a problem though: nobody used them and that — as we know from Ludwig Wittgenstein — made them meaningless.

The reference architectures weren't really used for a couple of reasons. The main reason was that it was impossible for any architect in a change initiative to know all these rules and take them all into account when making design decisions. Which project would allow the architect to spend (costly) time to read and learn these thousands of pages? And even if the architect would have read it all, a set of rules and regulations of this size is definitely going to be full of contradictions. The poor architect, confronted with a decision to be made, must do 'A' because of binder three, 'B' because of binder twelve, and sadly 'A' and 'B' contradict each other. The enterprise architects who created the rules, knowing that many exceptions would arise, and — being aware that blindly following a rule might sometimes lead to very unwanted consequences — made matters worse by often stating their rules with a large amount of leeway in one form or another. The poor project architect was thus left with a jungle of not always very strict and open to interpretation rules of which he or she had to decide how to use them. Most simple for that architect to get anything done: ignore them.[14]

When organizations started to realize that these huge sets of rules (principles and guidelines) were unusable and thus meaningless, a counter-movement ensued. On enterprise architecture conferences, speaker after speaker announced that organizations should not try to create and use hundreds of rules, but instead select roughly ten or so 'basic' or 'foundational' rules to guide change initiatives. Such a limited set of course solves the knowledge problem for the project architect who has to comply. But even after more than ten years of this approach, we still see the same chaos everywhere, so it clearly doesn't solve the problem either. The main reason is that these 'high level guidelines' are far too abstract and — indeed — high level to have a deciding effect on the actual low-level choices that create the chaos in the first place. Besides, the small set of rules cannot be interpretation-free, which leads to them being not very 'directive'.

The situation was even worse, because these high-level rules often weren't usable design rules at all. An often seen rule like "Reuse, before buy, before build" is, for instance, based on several questionable assumptions. Personally, I know of almost no more damaging architecture*▸ principle than this one. That M€150 disaster of the Dutch government agency* was for a large part the result of following this principle, as they started out (re)using tools without actually establishing if these formed a robust solution together[†].

In short: a set of principles is either a too large set of narrow rules, or a small set of overly broad rules. The first is unusable because of its size, the second is unusable because of the unspecificity of its rules, even if the rules itself are good. Both run foul of Wittgenstein's dictum, that can be stated as: "The meaning of a statement lies hidden in its correct use"[‡]. If there is no (correct) use, a statement is in essence meaningless. And thus, that shelf full of principles, guidelines, policies, exceptions, suggestions, all with their explanations had a limited meaning as there was limited correct use.

While principles and guidelines may be largely ineffective to solve the problems enterprise architecture has to solve, in practice their effect is often even negative. When coupled

---

One can argue if it really is an architecture principle, because 'buy' and 'build' are not architectural aspects of the resulting landscape, but matters of management. In fact, this principle has more to do with too simplistic ideas that exist in organizations about complexity and dreams about cost cutting than with sound architectural design.

See the start of chapter 1.

They didn't.

Actually, he never wrote it exactly like this. He wrote a lot about this issue, it is a core subject of his work, but what he wrote on this issue can be boiled down into this phrase. Note, it is not "meaning *is* use", as some have interpreted it. According to Wittgenstein, use *shows* meaning. The best explanation I know is P.M.S. Hacker's *Wittgenstein's place in 20th century analytic philosophy* [Hac96], but you can always go the the source, it is pretty readable.

with the governance rule 'comply or explain' — as is often done in enterprise architecture setups, because otherwise the principles can be too easily ignored by projects to count as 'principle' —, they may become particularly toxic. Those that create the principles are aware that there are always exceptions to the rule. Hence, they create the necessary leeway by stating 'comply or explain'*. There is, however, a fundamental problem with 'comply or explain'.

When projects are confronted with 'comply or explain', there is a hidden assumption — or maybe better: a hidden bias — that you cannot go wrong if you follow the principle (comply). Enterprise architects will say: "of course, otherwise it should not be a principle in the first place". We already noticed that the enterprise architects are aware that there are always exceptions to the rule, otherwise they would not try to govern by 'comply or explain'. The fact that you know there are exceptions means that you know it actually *can* be a bad thing to *follow* the principle. The bias of 'comply or explain', however, says otherwise. In other words: the use of 'comply or explain' is basically self-contradictory. The problem shows up, for instance, with project architects who are lazy, or who are good but unscrupulous and under a lot of time pressure, who will comply because it saves them trouble of going up against enterprise architecture. Project architects of a dubious quality will comply in cases where they really should not, because they do not know better.

If you give the principles but tell projects that they cannot blindly rely on them, project managers will complain loudly.

---

* Instead of 'comply or *die*', which the people responsible to keep the IT infrastructure running often long for.

Their drive, as we have seen before, is often largely directed at trying to corral certainties in an uncertain world, so principles that are not principles are against their drive to control scope as much as they can. From that perspective, using principles gets the full support of project managers and change departments in general[*].

If principles play a strong role in your enterprise architecture practice, a principle is thus often also followed, even when it is actually damaging to do so[†]. In my observations, it has been a main source of poor architecture and subsequent project failures. By the way, later I will argue that it is not wrong to have a couple of broad stroke design decisions (because that is what 'principles and guidelines' effectively are). But turning them into 'comply or explain'-principles is definitely risky business.

The trouble with domain 'know how'

When you need to make a design decision in your 'domain', you need to know that domain well. It is easy to make mistakes, overlook cases, make wrong assumptions if you do not know your domain well. So when an architect or designer creates a design in his or her domain, it is assumed that this designer knows the subject well.

But what happens when that design ends up at the central enterprise architecture function to be judged? Those enterprise architects do not have that domain knowledge at

---

[*] To be precise: until they find them inconvenient because of other project demands, such as time and budget.

[†] Hence, 'comply *and subsequently* die'...

all. So, how are they going to judge if the proposal makes good sense? Of course, they may have superior experience, recognize solutions or potential problems quickly, but that is all in a generic way. They do not know all the relevant details of that domain.

This ties in to another role that organizations often expect the enterprise architecture function to play. Every designer in a domain knows there is a lot more to the organization then what he or she knows. If your domain is accounting, you probably do not know all the ins and outs of domains that depend on accounting such as risk management, or reporting, to name a few. The organization often expects the enterprise architecture function to fill that gap*. The idea is that if a design is made in domain A, the designers there know everything about domain A and they can leave it to the central enterprise architecture function to check if the choices in their domain have deleterious effects on other domains.

The situation is thus twice problematic: not only do the central enterprise architects lack the domain knowledge to judge the proposals of the domain where the change takes place, they also lack the depth of knowledge to judge its knock-on effect on other domains. But the organization expects them to do both.

The result is that often in such a setup, the central enterprise architecture function becomes a low-quality bottleneck. To be able to judge the effect on their domains, they will have to go to those other domains in some way to ask them

---

* To get the 'coherence' across the organization's change initiatives that enterprise architecture is supposed to deliver.

their opinion based on their real insight and know how. The feedback then needs to be translated and transported again to the original designers, all in all a very inefficient and ineffective setup*. Alternatively, the central enterprise architecture function may stick to checking the design choices against set rules and regulations (the architecture 'principles'), trusting that following these is by definition good. And we already know that this doesn't really work either, or even may be very damaging.

Either way, the judgment is of low quality: the central enterprise architecture function sits in a knowledge position that makes it almost impossible for them to actually provide high-quality guidance. Instead of solving gaps, it forms a 'knowledge gap' in the organization.

The 'design office' alternative

An obvious solution to the 'knowledge gap' is to put all the architects in a single group. That way, it becomes easier to cooperate and share knowledge. The structure of the 'design office' setup of enterprise architecture in organizations is shown in figure 3.2 on page 56.

In this setup we get more 'design by collaboration' and domain know how is more readily available. But the setup introduces a couple of serious new problems. The first one is that you get multiple captains on each ship as the domain is responsible for the 'change' (e.g., a project) but the enterprise

---

In the worst case, you get poor enterprise architects, in a bad enterprise architecture setup, who are only busy passing issues and questions as hot potatoes to someone else.

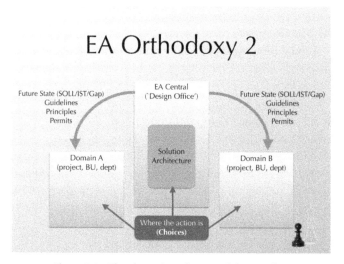

Figure 3.2 The alternative: the central design office

architecture function is responsible for the design of that change. Besides, there are more choices to be made than just the architectural design choices. These choices now are outside the operations of enterprise architecture as is illustrated in the figure. A second problem is that domains will not feel responsible for their own architecture, let alone feel a shared responsibility for the overall organization-wide architecture. All in all, the chance for conflicts is rather increased in this setup. This is also why it is often disbanded after a while.

So, the 'design office' variant of classic enterprise architecture solves a few problems, but introduces serious new problems in itself. It is better than nothing, but there is a better setup, as will be sketched later in the book.

Modeling strategy instead of enterprise

The 'essential enterprise design' school of enterprise architecture is the most prominent, but not the only one. Some see enterprise architecture above all as a governance subject, more a process than a content approach. And some see enterprise architecture as the discipline that translates policies into conceptual design decisions, which is a different kind of waterfall. That last aspect, the relation between enterprise strategy and enterprise architecture has grown over the last thirty years and these days, you'll find enterprise architects that are busy modeling strategies instead of enterprises.

Even the earliest enterprise architecture methods, such as the Zachman Framework* from the 1992 edition onwards, paid attention to the 'why' of enterprise architecture. The 1992 Zachman Framework, for instance, introduced a 'motivation' column, where for each of the roles it recognized (planner, owner, designer, builder, programmer†, user), there were six aspects of architecture (what, how, where, who, when, and *why*). The evolution of enterprise architecture methods towards more goal-oriented approaches has been reflected in the Zachman Framework, when the 'why' column of 1992 moved from the last column ('why' as an explanation) to the first column ('why' as a driver, a first step) as it still is today. Another example is the ArchiMate enterprise architecture language, which in version 2 (2012) got an

---

As Roger Sessions observed, it is more a taxonomy than a framework.
All of the enterprise architecture methods to date are strongly IT-centric. This is natural, because the complexities of IT have driven the development of these methods in the first place. Recently, other parts of the enterprise have come more in play, but most methods haven't caught up yet.

extension for modeling the motivation for an enterprise architecture, with elements like 'Driver', 'Goal', 'Requirement', 'Constraint' and 'Principle' amongst others.

In reality, the world of intentions of an organization is not only far more complex than can be reliably modeled as 'discrete' elements in a usable way. What is more, the real 'elements' that make up human motivations, drivers and such are seldom sharply defined, may overlap and have many hidden relations. Modeling just a few of these with only a few of the relations, then, is just another brittle oversimplification of reality. In practice, if these models are rich enough in detail to become even a bit meaningful, they become unmanageable. If they are simple (such as in any example given by the people who try to sell these modeling practices to us) there is little value of a model over just writing a few motivational items in a list. The situation mirrors the problems with the rules and principles approach for enterprise landscape development. It also is related to failed attempts to formally verify programs by tracing from requirements to design.[15]

The assumption that it is meaningful to model the complex, contradictory and overlapping world of human motivation in a web of discrete-like* elements and relations is reminiscent of early attempts at artificial intelligence: it all may look promising at small scale but dies of combinatorial explosion at any reasonable scale. Using structure to guide your strategic thinking is not wrong, but thinking that you can turn

---

* The model is discrete, the intended meaning of the elements and relations generally is not, but is vague, contradictory, *human*.

this structure into decisions is. Only in very simple cases does this work*. But organizations are never simple.

Are you an architect? Really?

Enterprise architecture is often compared to architecture in the physical world, the world of buildings, bridges, cities and neighborhoods. If this comparison is made, the 'IT system' (and all that comes with it such as processes for its use) that is to be implemented is often seen as the 'house'. The enterprise architects then see themselves as a kind of 'city planners', setting the overall rules for all house developments, drawing up plans for neighborhoods, et cetera.[16] In many ways, this is a usable analogy, but it also has a couple of fundamental weaknesses that lie at the heart of the problems of enterprise architecture.

First, when you want to build a *real* bridge across a river, you first go to the banks of that river and you investigate. You research the condition of the underground, you look at the environment and so forth. Having done all that, you return to the office and you create a design. You can take a year if you want to; that river is not going anywhere. When the design is ready and approved — a year or two later — you return with your contractor and all his personnel and materials and you build the bridge.

---

* There is some scientific evidence for this in psychological research that shows that conscious (and thus more explicit) methods for decision making only work in cases where there are only a few simple aspects, say around three. Above that, afterwards people tend to be less satisfied with their decision than those who made the decision without actually making their arguments and reasoning explicit. See [Dij06].

In IT-for-the-Business, however, the situation is quite different. First, it is difficult enough in most cases to actually find the 'banks' of the 'river'*. And what is worse: if you return even only three months later, those 'banks' have already shifted elsewhere[†].

There is something else wrong with the city planner analogy, not so much the analogy itself, but with the way the enterprise architecture 'orthodoxy' positions itself in it. In the organizations that do enterprise level architecture[‡], most follow a definition of architecture like the one from ISO/IEC/IEEE 42010 from 2011 we encountered earlier (see page 45):

Architecture: fundamental concepts or properties of a system in its environment embodied in its elements, relationships, and in the principles of its design and evolution

This widely used definition says two things. Architecture is 'what is' and 'how it should evolve'. The 'what is' is not explicit, by the way, the first part could apply to a 'to be' architecture as well. But the whole phrase suggests the first

---

* Many systems have to deal with human behavior and requirements (the 'ethical' ones are the worst) that is not really all that clear from the start. The intended system will likely also have to integrate with many other systems, and the requirements of these are not exactly known at the start as well.

[†] Not so much because of IT's rapid change, as many think, but more because of the volatility of human enterprise.

[‡] In many enterprises, enterprise architects are forced to run from project to project, never being allowed to look at the enterprise level. Frankly, those organizations may employ what they call 'enterprise architects', but they are not doing 'enterprise architecture' by any standard. Architects in these enterprises often envy the ones that are allowed to do enterprise architecture at the actual enterprise level.

part is about the current state. The second part is explicit. It says architecture is about the *principles* of design and evolution.

These principles are meant to have two effects: prevent the chaos and direct ourselves to a better world. Architecture is seen as something that limits the freedom of those that design the changes. In the Dutch enterprise architecture world, this is phrased as 'kaderstellend voor ontwerp', a phrase that translates a bit like 'setting the boundaries for design'. All in all, the idea that architecture is a set of rules that *govern* design (and thus is not design itself) is embedded deeply in our discipline.[17] Enterprise architects feel way above (IT) designers. They feel they are the 'directors of design'.

But if we go back to the world of cities and buildings, creating sets of rules is not what architects do at all. Architects in the real world make *designs*. Architects of the physical design practical structures, anything from bus shelters to large buildings, or even city plans. And in the case of buildings, their designs will include relevant details such as where the wall sockets are located (as these influence the usability of the building.

Actually, principles have been influential as guiding instruments for physical architecture: after World War II. This has not really worked out. In the world of cities and buildings, the principle-based rational and utopian city architectures* have led to many urban disasters, such as crime-infested high-rise housing projects. The principles were arguably beautiful, the result of applying them for design often was a disaster[†]. Still,

---

E.g., as put forward in the Athens Charter by Le Corbusier.
A lesson for enterprise architecture if there ever was one.

even those principle-oriented architects did not just produce principles (the 'boundaries for design'), they produced actual designs that embedded those principles.

In the world of cities and houses there is one type of governance that actually works via 'boundaries for design'. Those rules are set by the government, and they will be about societal values such as safety, environment, health, access for the physically handicapped, and such. These values are translated to building rules in a *building decree*. These boundaries are enforced by the *building inspector*. Architects of the physical are clearly not building inspectors, but, strangely enough, the role of 'governing design through rules', the role of the building inspector, is exactly the position many enterprise architects have maneuvered themselves into. And their products reflect that. In some versions of templates for project start architectures, such as the current one from Sogeti's DYA enterprise architecture framework, we even see *nothing but* principles and guidelines.

When you are designing or building something physical, the building inspectors come along and see if the design of the architect (or the implementation by the contractor) is within those limits, thus fulfilling the intention of protecting society against problems like 'a race to the bottom' with respect to those values. As the whole of these rules are often experienced as overzealous and impractical meddling with development freedom, building inspectors are not very popular.

This mirrors why it is often so difficult for the business to truly value what enterprise architects do. That is because the product of principle-oriented enterprise architects is not a recognizable contribution to the end result at all. Their product sets up *limitations* (or utopian ideas) for the contribution, but it is *not a contribution* to the solution itself. These 'architects' do not produce an architecture at all, they produce something resembling a mix between a building decree* and the utopian principles of the modernist architects of the 20's and 30's of the previous century. And they are thus not like architects in the physical world at all, they are more like a mix of utopian city planners (with principles, but without the plan†) and building inspectors. They are also about as popular as the latter.

In short: the mode of operation that overly uses principles and guidelines not only does not work well, it actually turns architecture into something that is not architecture at all. An 'architecture' should not (negatively) be a set of limitations, not 'boundaries for design', it should *positively* describe (a design) what the solutions are to be. Not in all detail, of course, only *relevant* detail is to be added as we noticed before. This is true in the physical world as well. The architect in the physical world will probably not describe the floor color‡, but the location of wall sockets *is* significant, and so it is described. This architecture must conform to the (building decree, amongst others) requirements instead of being requirements. When the architecture for a project

---

In which they act as both law maker and inspector, which makes other stakeholders in the enterprise feel suspicious to boot.

Or if they have a plan, it is often an explicit future state that never comes to pass because of the uncertainties and volatilities of the enterprise architecture game.

That is for the decorator, in Dutch called the 'interior-architect'*▶

is completed, it must be clear for the builder what is to be built.

In other words: an architecture must be a tangible contribution to the end result, instead of something of which the value is so far removed from the actual issues that nobody (except the enterprise architect) recognizes it as a 'constructive contribution' anymore. Rules in the physical architecture world, like building decrees or the utopian city-planning principles of Le Corbusier, do not lead to good designs by themselves. In the case of building decrees, they are generally offshoots of the societal values behind them, often guarding minimum requirements against the (cost- and time-saving) pressures of the market. Rules (principles, guidelines) in enterprise architecture should be likewise. A quote from the architect Thomas Reid applies: "The rules of navigation never navigated a ship. The rules of architecture never built a house."

So, to be an enterprise architect, ones products should be actual designs that contribute directly to the results, instead of only setting limitations on the results. A *design* of a landscape to build*. A *design* of the end result of a project. Note, this does not mean architects are to be like the 'enterprise architect' mentioned at the beginning, the one running from independent project to independent project and never taking the 'enterprise' view.

If someone's products, on the other hand, are made up mainly of limitations (principles, guidelines, policies and

*◄ My, o my, how we love the title 'architect'...

* With limitations, as detailed long term future states descriptions are not very useful. We need something else, see in chapter 6.

such), he should call himself 'visionary enterprise inspector'*, but not enterprise 'architect'.[18]

Why do we do it the way we do it?

If you look at all the problems with the classic approach to enterprise architecture, you have to wonder why we do it that way at all. Personally, I think there are both deep cultural and psychological reasons why we try it in a way that so clearly has serious limitations. The next chapter will show why our current 'best practices' of enterprise architecture are so ineffective, and also why we keep on trying to use them anyway.

Meanwhile, at the university

For a subject that is over thirty years old, there is pretty little empirical proof that *any* of the proposed methods of frameworks actually work. It is of course a pretty difficult area for measurements to be made. You need very large statistical research based on huge amounts of what is clearly company-sensitive information to do it. Without a huge database, how will you be able to weed out other effects? After all, if the project was a success, how can you say it was enterprise architecture that made it a success and not, say, project management? And if the company was successful, how do we know it was the enterprise architecture that was key to

---

It was the best I could come up with, and yes: it is the worst of both worlds.

that success and not, say, market events or just plain luck? And even if we would have this database, how do we make a database of real comparable numbers and not — unreliable — opinions*? And if we would have this database and we could weed out some statistical *descriptive* correlations, how would we know they are causal *prescriptive* relations?

So, what we are left with are a lot of 'white papers', generally from non-neutral sources, such as system or methodology vendors. What passes for science in this field is often based on laughably small samples, from which grand conclusions are drawn, which are subsequently quoted in other industry papers. There are peer-review published articles (quoted in such white papers) which are based on interviews with only a few companies.

Enterprise architecture is not unique in that hard evidence is difficult to find. Management theories are in the same boat, even the most popular ones. Try to find proof that *using* Porter's famous five-forces model actually works to make better strategy. At least the theories of management may often have some basis in empirical research (Porter's had), even if — as far as I know —there is no proof that using them helps. For enterprise architecture, the theories and frameworks themselves are generally dreamed up by

---

* After all, these are not just opinions (which have some use in a statistical setting), they are often *uninformed* opinions. I have often seen exactly the wrong conclusions drawn from failure; such as organizations concluding the problem was in project management, or user behavior, while the real cause of failure lay in uninformed poor architectural choices such as choosing to use a combination of two platforms that were fundamentally incompatible at the technical level.

individuals or small groups based on personal convictions, let alone that their effect is reliably measured.

Lost in detail

Finally, there is one aspect of current 'state of the art' methodologies that merits a remark. Frameworks like TOGAF and FEAF are huge, they are easily many hundreds of pages in size. FEAF, for instance, is over 400 hundred large pages, TOGAF 9.1 is available in a 654 page paperback. The ballooned size of these frameworks is reminiscent of the ballooned 'reference architectures' of the past, only worse: these are enormous descriptions on *how* to get architectural results, not the required potentially useful real architectural choices themselves. How executable or understandable for an organization is a method for enterprise architecture that requires so much information to describe? How usable (and thus meaningful) are they? How much effort do you need to follow the framework's guidelines before you are actually doing any useful architecture work that is specific for your organization?

It is rather ironic that enterprise architecture frameworks, their followers generally preaching a 'fundamentals' or 'high-level' approach to design, consist of hundreds of pages of often inconsistent* detail.

Such as the different definitions of concepts like 'function' or 'capability' that can be found within TOGAF's hundreds of pages.

*Henri the painter was not French and his name
was not Henri. Also he was not really a painter*
John Steinbeck — *Cannery Row*

Intermezzo:
A Short Story about Grief

LET ME tell you a little story. There was once a young man who dreamed of reducing the world to pure logic. Because he was a very clever young man, he actually managed to do it. When he had finished his work, he stood back and admired it. It was beautiful! A world purged of imperfection and indetermenency. Countless acres of gleaming ice stretching to the horizon. So the clever young man looked around the world he had created and decided to explore it. He took one step forward and fell flat on his back. You see, he had forgotten about friction! The ice was smooth and level and stainless, but you couldn't walk there. So the clever young man sat down and wept bitter tears. But as he grew into a wise old man, he came to understand that roughness and ambiguity aren't imperfections, they are what make the world turn. He wanted to run and dance. And the words and things scattered upon the ground were all battered and tarnished and ambiguous. The wise old man saw that that was the way things were. Something in him was still homesick for the ice, where everything was radiant and absolute and relentless. Though he had come to like the idea of the rough ground, he couldn't bring himself to live there. So now he was marooned between earth and ice, at home at neither. And this was the cause of all his grief."

— From the Terry Eagleton script for the movie *Wittgenstein*.

Nowadays the dynamic element is more important in chess — players more often sacrifice material to obtain dynamic compensation
Boris Spassky

4 Chess

A S WAS MENTIONED on page 45, the — in enterprise architecture circles most often quoted — ANSI/IEEE Std
1471-2000 standard says architecture is about the broad
strokes and the rules that direct and guide actual design;
and this is often explained to the business by using the 'city
planner' analogy for enterprise architect. But, as was illustrated in the previous chapter, if your target is to establish
good houses, you know, houses that actually 'work' for their
inhabitants* — that are easy to maintain, cheap to heat, can
be used flexibly, et cetera —, then having 'city plans' or
'neighborhood plans' or 'street maps' is not going to make a
big difference. In fact, the thing is that city planners do have
surprisingly little bearing on the houses themselves.

As far as I am concerned, the concept of enterprise
architecture being like 'city planning' and as 'above design'
is one of the reasons why enterprise architecture so seldom
succeeds. We are looking at it in a fundamentally wrong
manner. For me, the game of chess is a far better analogy
for what we enterprise architects should do, as chess shares
many aspects of the situation enterprise architects experience
every day. Let's illustrate.

Une maison est une machine-à-habiter. (A house is a machine for living
in.) – Le Corbusier

Making a move

When in chess a player makes a move, he* does not have an exact end position in mind. It is not as if a player thinks: "I will work towards the following *exact* checkmate position: his king on position x, his pawn on position y, my queen on position z, et cetera". In other words: chess players do not make moves with a well-defined end-state in mind†. They do not even work with an *approximate* end position in mind. Chess players evaluate moves as to what they improve in their overall *current* situation.

Opposite to chess players, most enterprise architects often start out with some 'future state architecture' and then try to invent moves (and guidelines for moves) that will let the enterprise evolve to that state. They tend to live their life backwards; instead of working forward from the current state, they put themselves in an imagined future state and then look back to the current state. In the field of strategy, this approach is called 'backcasting'. The problem with that approach is that the real world enterprise architects play in is very unpredictable and volatile, just like chess. All kinds of unexpected developments take place, and the dreamed future state generally never comes to pass. Only if you create

---

* Normally I take care to write 'he or she' but that will become very tedious in this part. Given that both in enterprise architecture and chess men are in an overwhelming majority (for reasons outside the scope of this little book) I will use male pronouns here and my apologies for all the women who are active in either chess or enterprise architecture. In my experience most of you do not really mind or you do not even register this, but I did not want it to go unmentioned.

† Except in the absolute final moves of the game.

your architecture at a very high abstraction level, it may be. But in that case, you can wonder how discriminating that future state actually is, and how much it will be able to direct developments and get you your goals.

But the question is, of course, how much does this 'backcasting'-approach solve the problems, mentioned on page 38, that enterprise is required to solve? Not so much, as it has turned out over the last decennia. So, instead of living their life backwards, maybe enterprise architects should live their life *forwards*, as if they were chess players, with each change in the Business-IT landscape seen as a move in an 'enterprise chess' game.

Chess players evaluate potential moves in many ways. They will try to find the best move that gives them (potential) material advantage, doesn't expose them to risks too much, increase the robustness of their position, et cetera.

Enterprise architects want to use principles and guidelines to get the best evolution of their landscape. What do chess players have in terms of such tactical rules to guide the evolution of their game?

Tactical rules

When my young son had learnt the basics of chess, he asked me: "I know what moves are allowed, what the rules* are. But when is a move a *good* move? What are the rules for

---

Game rules in chess, such as 'a rook must move vertically or horizontally', may be compared to aspects of enterprise architecture such as 'you cannot send a cup of coffee via the internet'. In this section we are discussing 'tactical rules', the rules of making *good* moves, not just legal ones.

that?"*. So, I gave him a few rules. For instance, I said: "Suppose you take pieces from your opponent and he takes some back. You can calculate easily if it is a profitable exchange. You give a queen 9 points, a rook 5, a bishop and a knight 3, and a pawn 1. If you take more points from him than he takes from you, it is a profitable exchange".[19]

In chess, however, such a tactical rule is not 'prescriptive' but 'descriptive'. This requires an explanation. A 'prescriptive rule' is a rule that you must/can follow. It 'prescribes' certain behavior. But in chess, following a rule like the one above about exchange of material with points for each type of piece does not make you win games, the complexity of the game is much higher than can be solved with a reasonably sized set of such simple rules. Follow a rule like this in all situations, and your opponent will trap you; offering a piece to get tactical advantage is a common strategy in chess.

But what you *will* see is that if you analyze *many* games *after they have completed*, the winner will in almost all cases during the game have gained material advantage[†]. The rule may not be very useful in a 'prescriptive' way, but it certainly describes an aspect of the outcome well, in a *descriptive* statistical manner[‡]. It 'describes' something that generally

---

* Not literally of course, but it boiled down to this.
† Often as a result of threatening to get an even more advantageous *material* advantage.
‡ This is comparable to the difference between statistical and causal relationships. Going back to the remark on scientific evidence for existing methods in the previous chapter: Porter may have found empirical evidence for his five-forces model, that does not mean the result is usable as *causal* relations.

happens when a game is played well. It is a 'rule' in the phrase "as a rule ..."*.

There are many such descriptive rules that can be found about how chess winners played their game. Winners developed their pieces better, they had robustness in their positions (they defended their pieces well), they attacked where the opposition was weak and so forth.

If, instead, you want to play chess with 'prescriptive rules', you need a really big computer (and possibly a bit of cheating), as the matches between then world chess champion Gary Kasparov and a specialized IBM chess supercomputer in the 90's of the previous century showed.[20] Ignoring the influence of the team of humans involved on IBM's side, the match between Deep Blue and Kasparov tells us something about the amount of 'prescriptive rules' (because that is how a digital computer works[†]) you need to beat human estimation, even in a clearly logical domain as chess. Working on the basis of 'prescriptive rules' requires an enormous amount of them to be somewhat intelligent, and that is even without a learning capability.

If you ask me, enterprise architects should work with their principles and guidelines like a chess player works with tactical rules. Above all, they should not be followed blindly as a Law of the Medes and Persians. The popular approach of principles and guidelines as a *foundation* of an enterprise

---

This ties in closely to what Wittgenstein has written on rules and rule-following.

Though this may be artfully hidden by using techniques such as digital neural networks, which look like they are not based on prescriptive rules, but they are. The rules are well hidden, but they are there. A neural network on a digital computer is a *data-driven rule-based system in disguise*.[21]

architecture is as fundamentally mistaken as it would be to base a game of chess on trying to follow all the named tactical rules you can remember simultaneously and consciously*. It is just as with the toxicity of 'comply or explain' mentioned on page 52: you *can* go wrong following a rule that is in itself not bad, and you must *also* explain if you *do* follow the rule, not just when you do *not* follow it. The rule is 'descriptive' and not 'prescriptive'.[22]

A good chess player does not follow the rules, the rules are 'embedded' in his skill without being exactly visible during play. For enterprise architects the same must be true: *the architect should not be governed by the rules, the rules should be an (invisible) part of the architect's skills.*

Sometimes, a pawn is decisive

Many enterprise architects loathe details. For them, details are for (IT) engineers, a rather lowly form of corporate life if you look at how enterprise architects often treat them[†]. In the current 'best practice' of enterprise architecture, therefore, the idea of '*significant* aspects' has been without protest changed into the concept '*fundamental* aspects' and these are seen as the 'high-level' ones[‡].

But the devil is in the details, as the saying goes. The Chinese proverb from Confucius is particularly effective to

---

* That you cannot play chess based on deploying only a *few* simple rules is obvious too.
† Engineers often experience the high-brow enterprise architects as pretty arrogant, you may imagine, and this doesn't help the enterprise architects to build influence.
‡ See for instance ISO/IEC/IEEE 42010.[23]

make that point: "Men do not stumble over mountains, but over molehills". The enterprise architect has his mountain perfectly targeted in his crosshairs, but the enterprise never even hits that mountain because it has stumbled over a neglected molehill long before it gets to its goal. This happens constantly in enterprise architecture. No wonder organizations remain skeptical about the value of enterprise architecture.

The problem is, however, not specific for enterprise architecture, it is a more generic aspect of how we approach issues. In 1964, journalist Sidney J. Harris wrote:

> In every field of inquiry, it is true that all things should be made as simple as possible — but no simpler.

This has become a popular saying[24], but Harris added a bracketed sentence that is seldom mentioned:

> (And for every problem that is muddled by over-complexity, a dozen are muddled by over-simplifying).

And this is true for enterprise architecture as well. Over-simplifying (ignoring details, instead of taking *significant* details into account) is the name of the game in many enterprise architecture circles, where (as mentioned above) details are seen as the domain of the (lowly) engineers, and where 'architecture' is not 'design'. An enterprise architect who gives attention to detail is generally not well-received in enterprise architecture circles, where it is considered 'bad form' to go into detail. Harris was right: over-simplification is far more prevalent than over-complication. In enterprise architecture, a world of many complex dependencies, often deep in the details, it is also much more dangerous.

Besides, a person may stumble, but right himself and go on without actually falling down. The effect of ignoring details in a nondiscriminatory fashion in enterprise architecture are often far worse. You may end up in a completely unworkable landscape where you need all kinds of workarounds and inefficiencies to get anything done. It is therefore often the case that, in enterprise architecture, the road to landscape hell (and failed projects) is based on grand over-simplified designs.

The situation is likewise in chess. Details count. Some-times, the fact that that lowly pawn is just one square more forward may open or close up entire scenarios; in some cases it may even determine the difference between winning and losing. In chess you *cannot* ignore details, you must pay attention to the *relevant* (or *significant*) ones and there are no simple rules to decide which are relevant. The same is true in enterprise architecture. The question of course is how to do that, because — as with chess — paying attention to *all* the details is clearly beyond our human capabilities* and we need a smart way to find the relevant ones. We will return to the question of handling details in enterprise architecture in chapter 5.

The chess player

So, how do good chess players handle all that complexity and unpredictability in chess? We as enterprise architects might learn from their example.

---

* Dijkstra: "The competent programmer is fully aware of the strictly limited size of his own skull" [Dij72]. This holds for enterprise architects even more than for programmers.

Clearly chess players do not evaluate *all* the details and they do not work towards a well-defined end situation. In a seminal work *Het denken van den schaker. Een experimenteel-psychologische studie**, which got him a cum laude doctorate in psychology, Adriaan de Groot described in 1946 the thought processes of chess players. He did extensive experiments, one of which was giving both grand masters and amateurs positions[26] and then recording how they vocalized their thoughts while they were thinking about a next move to make. De Groot discovered a few important aspects. For instance, he found out that — surprisingly — amateurs and grand master are alike in the number of alternatives they study. Where grand masters and amateurs differed was in the 'orientation phase'; grand masters were much better at *focusing on the right area* of the board *before* starting to look for alternatives (the 'exploration phase') and analyzing these. Grand masters also did not overlook the right moves, whereas amateurs often did not spot these as promising and subsequently forgot to take these into account in their calculations. In short: masters had superior *pattern recognition*, not superior *calculation*.

So, what would constitute a non-amateur enterprise architect? Well, this person must have the characteristics of a chess professional with respect to the way he comes to design decisions. Het must be good at orientation: finding the places in the Business-IT landscape where moves need or can be made. He must not overlook the best moves. He must of course also be good at modeling, as modeling is for enterprise architecture what calculating is for chess.

Later translated into English as *Thought and Choice in Chess [DG08].*[25]

An enterprise architect does not need to be an expert in an enterprise architecture framework. Though frameworks have useful parts and insights, they are poor substitutes for insight into the complexities and peculiarities of an enterprise landscape*, even if some structure and a good governance setup (which we'll discuss in chapter 5) obviously benefits the enterprise architecture trade. An enterprise architect needs to be able to have a strategic outlook, just as the chess grand master. Because, though the chess grand master concentrates on making good moves (tactics), a chess grand master often also has a strategy. He has a vision that guides his moves. In enterprise architecture, that vision is called the Future State Architecture (or FSA for short). The 'future state' will be discussed in chapter 6.

The (very) bad news

Humans can play chess, that much is clear. And if enterprise architecture is like chess, a human may 'play enterprise architecture' as well, right? Sadly, no, because chess, as an analogy for the enterprise is not perfect: complex as chess is, compared to enterprise architecture chess is really, really, *really* simple. If you, in comparison, look at the enterprise compared to a game of chess you will get the feeling that enterprise architecture is an *impossible* endeavor for a human. After all:

---

* And often their basic premises about doing enterprise architecture — such as principle-driven design — are questionable, as argued in this book. I have always quite liked the original basic approach of the DYA framework, though. It is pragmatic and focuses a lot on the importance of 'making a move' well. More recently, it seems to have lost that focus.

- In chess, you can *perfectly* know your position before deciding on a move. There are only 64 squares and a maximum of 32 pieces*. In the enterprise, however, it is practically impossible to know the entire landscape with all its details.† As mentioned before: compared to building a bridge, in enterprise architecture you cannot even clearly see the banks of the river. The 'chess board' of the enterprise is orders of magnitude larger than a real chess board and it is impossible to know everything that is on it when you have to decide on a move. To make matters worse: the 'squares' of the enterprise chess board are not clearly separated, they overlap;
- The 'freedom of choice' is much more limited in chess than in the enterprise. There are only so much possible legal moves in any chess situation. De Groot estimated that there are on average 32 possible legal moves every time a player must make one. Compared to the freedom and number of choices in enterprise architecture when you are designing a change in the landscape, this is probably a very small number, or, in other words:

Of only six 'types'. And over the life time of the game the number decreases, in the Business-IT landscape it often increases.

And many attempts to actually know the whole board before deciding on a move end in 'analysis paralysis'. Note that it is possible to know more than the usual 'almost nothing', and a good current state architecture (see appendix B) will definitely help. Note also that knowing the landscape very well within the scope of a change initiative is also possible. But to *judge* the change initiative, more of the board has to be taken into account than the scope of the initiative itself. The architectural scope is always wider than project scope, and forgetting that is a common pitfall.

a chess move is a simple change compared to an enterprise architecture change*.

The situation is even more difficult for most enterprises because the 'moves' themselves are often more complex than the simple moves in chess:

— While in chess, every move can be made independently, in the enterprise, it is often impossible to make one move without making also another move at the same time;

— Organizations do not build all their software themselves. These days, much of what they use is *bought*. And what they buy has not been tailored perfectly to their wishes. In terms of architecture, they are not realizing their architecture, they are buying pieces of *canned architecture* from vendors.

For instance, you may want risk management software that can be fed via your existing integration method, e.g., an enterprise service bus, but if the only software that satisfies the business requirements on risk calculations can only be fed with flat files and by starting a command line program on a server, you end up integrating it in that archaic way. It is as if you want to move a rook in chess but some bishop will also move automatically if you move that rook.

The latter, by the way, highlights a common problem with many enterprise architecture approaches, where

---

* De Groot also estimated that at every turn there were only a very small number of *good* moves, maybe three or four. Many legal moves are easily to be seen very bad, so the chess master only really contemplates a very small number of options for every move. The art is to recognize the three or four potentially good moves *before* analyzing them.

the whole approach was originally based on the idea that the framework was meant to steer software *development*, not *purchase*. People think they first define an architecture (consisting of rules like "we always use the enterprise service bus", "infrastructure cost may not scale in excess of the logarithm of the number of users") and then make it happen. But unless you develop everything yourself, you do not have that freedom; you are at the mercy of the few providers that can fulfill some essential business requirements.

- And not only is it impossible to know your position perfectly, in enterprise architecture it changes while you're thinking of a move. And to make matters worse: in the enterprise, if you have designed your move and you start implementing it (changes and projects) the position will change *while* you are thinking or moving and those are not changes you initiate yourself, but they come from unexpected sources.

- Worse even: in chess all the unpredictability is created by that single opponent* and both of you move taking clear turns. Not so in the enterprise: there are many players all making moves (changes) *simultaneously* on that same gigantic chess board; they're not taking turns

---

* When telling this story to people, I have often been asked: if chess is the analogy, who are you fighting against in enterprise architecture? The answer is that in enterprise architecture we are fighting unpredictability and unknowability. The opponent in the chess analogy stands mainly for the unpredictability we are fighting in enterprise architecture. To be clear: the opponent's role in chess is not that important in the analogy, not everything in chess can be translated to enterprise architecture. There are, as Protagoras[27] and Wittgenstein would have said, only *resemblances*.

and often they don't play nice and follow any agreed 'game rules'.

- And finally, the strategic goal of chess is rather simple — checkmate the opponent — but the strategic goals of the organization are complex, vague, and sometimes even internally contradictory; and some of the goals may come from the outside (lawmakers, regulators). To top it off, the goals change during the game, not once but multiple times and there is no end to the game[*].

In short: chess is extremely simple: there are only 64 unambiguous squares, there are just 6 discrete types of piece, there are clear and simple strictly logical game rules, and you and your opponent neatly take turns and act in a civilized manner, whereas enterprises are largely political environments and not only governed by the official rules, but also by the unwritten rules[†]. Even with all that simplicity, chess is already an endeavour that cannot be predictably executed towards a set goal. Enterprise architecture, therefore, is *The Chess Game from Hell*; its complexity is many orders of magnitude higher than chess[‡]. No wonder we fail at attaining its objectives with mechanisms that resemble those that do not even work

---

[*] Unless the organization itself ends, such as a government agency shutting down or a business going bankrupt.

[†] The insights and ideas in Peter Scott-Morgan's book *The Unwritten Rules of the Game* [SM94] can be enlightening in this respect.

[‡] One thing that is easier in the enterprise is that it is allowed to redo a move: you can stop the faltering project and start over again. This, however, is not a preferred state of affairs, and comes with its own added complex problems, such as the effects of running late with certain important required changes.

in the limited complexity of chess, let alone the complexity of real organizations.

Why do we do it the way we do it?

So, in the light of the obvious impossibility of the standard enterprise architecture setup to work, why do so many enterprise architects and their employers believe in the effectiveness of future state models, principles and guidelines? Why is so massively believed and practiced that a few simple rules and an abstract future state is going to solve our complexity problem? Why is it the core of most enterprise architecture practices? Why, after thirty years, is nobody shouting that the emperor is not wearing clothes? There is a simple answer for that: it is *seductive*; we *want* to believe in them. There are both cultural and psychological/biological reasons to want to believe them.

On the psychological/biological side we, as humans with our limited capabilities, are confronted with the realization that the complexity of the real organization is way beyond our capability as a human to digest, and we are deeply convinced that what we *must* do — manage the landscape (in its full complexity, because we *are* aware that details may make or break our plans) — *cannot be done* at all. In that situation, we feel powerless, which is a major psychological/-biological stress factor in humans.

Humans, as so many animals, when confronted with stress have three built-in biological options: fight, flight and freeze. The way we embrace the simple answers to the complex problems of enterprise architecture can be considered a 'flight' reaction. We do not confront complexity, we do not freeze up and hope it goes away*, but we run away from it to a make-believe simplified world where life is not complex beyond our capabilities, where we can reliably plan and feel 'in control'. The belief in that clear future state and those understandable and simple principles and guidelines, gives us the idea that we are not powerless at all, and this is an extremely seductive psychological state. It is a form of 'wishful thinking'.[†]

The simple future state landscapes that are presented to higher management also play into this psychological need. When enterprise architects present their clean and abstract views of the future landscape to higher management, higher management becomes enthusiastic. After all, that future landscape looks far more simple and manageable than the current chaos, the effects of which they feel every day (especially when they want changes and it turns out that changing the landscape is very complex, and thus costly and risky). Which board member would not want to exchange the semi-chaotic reality for the clean future state the enterprise architects sketch? Sadly, the cleanliness is a seductive figment of the imagination. People seldom realize that *every* landscape, *even the current chaotic one* looks very clean and simple when abstracted enough.

---

[*] Though in some organizations you will see this behavior for short periods.
[†] The behavior of classical enterprise architecture is also reminiscent of that old joke about the drunk looking for his lost keys under a street light. When asked by the passing cop what he is doing, he says: "I'm looking for my keys". The cop asks: "Did you lose them here?". "No", says the drunk, "I lost them back there". "So why are you looking for them here, then?" asks the policeman? "Well", says the drunk, "here is the light".

Another flight behavior is hiding in plain sight. Confronted with the fact that a major goal of enterprise architecture is effectively also to handle *future and unknown* requirements*, existing enterprise architecture practices all silently turn them into — current and known — *expectations* about the future. You find two types of behavior of this switch in the enterprise architecture context. Some force themselves to believe the expectations as truths, and they diligently work toward that 'certain' goal. Others know in the back of their mind that the future cannot be predicted, and they only pay lip service to the idea of a future state. In chapter 6 we will see that there is a way to manage the uncertainties of the future in a better way.

The enterprise architects, who are (in part subconsciously) aware that the complexity is beyond what is manageable from a human standpoint and partly unpredictable to boot, may flee in simplicity and the 'now'. But many in the organization are not even aware the extreme complexity is there in the first place, for them the make-believe simplicity seems real. This is a real Catch-22 for enterprise architecture. Enterprise architects that present extremely simplified pictures of reality to management that management likes actually work against their own need to get management properly aware of the actual complexity problem. Presenting simplified views of the hideously complex reality to management supports management in any existing belief that enterprise architecture (or IT) is in essence simple.[28] The abstractions enterprise architects employ effectively hide the complexity they are trying to manage out of sight. This also creates a fertile ground

_____
See page 38

for belief in architecture patterns such as service oriented architectures and cloud computing* as 'silver bullets'.

The love of simplified make-believe landscapes is also a driver for the often seen 'enterprise architecture board room game', a very — obviously — *simple* game played like this:

Step 1: An enterprise architecture initiative is (re-)started;

Step 2: The enterprise architects present a simplified future state architecture and a simple set of principles and guide-lines to the board[†]. The board embraces these, satisfied as they are with its (illusion of) simplicity and it presenting a feeling of being 'in control';

Step 3: Between one-and-a-half and three years later, the board has become dissatisfied. Projects complain about enterprise architecture's lack of value and the chaos it is supposed to stop has not disappeared. Back to square 1.

One reason this game is played over and over again has to do with the limited depth of 'organizational memory'. In the management of many an organization, changes of 'who does what' happen at such a regular basis that it is difficult for the organization to experience the strong sense of déjà-vu for things that change every three years or so. To experience déjà-vu, one needs to have experienced it two or three times in a row.

On the cultural side: we live in a culture that strongly believes in the power of logical reasoning as being the most powerful reasoning of all. This started with philosophers

---

* See appendix A

[†] And if any, a *simple* set of governance rules.

in antiquity[*] who laid the foundation for this culture when they started to use discrete logical reasoning (based on the true/false dichotomy). There is much more to be said about this, but as Hubert Dreyfus so beautifully showed when he discussed the unfounded belief of early cognitive science and artificial intelligence researchers in their logical foundations[†], we are living in a culture of 2500 years that assumes that logical reasoning trumps everything else. We tend to think rule-like mechanisms are also effective in those places where they are not. In Hubert Dreyfus' case it was artificial intelligence. In this case it is classical enterprise architecture, where using logical rules (principles and guidelines) fits our (misguided) idea of intelligent behavior like a glove.

The low status of IT

In the eyes of the business, IT is generally not seen as a stellar performer. IT projects are often over budget, late, and without providing the promised results in full. Every disturbance of smooth operations is considered a failure. Combatting disturbances with double or even triple backups leads to very high cost and disturbances still happen[‡].

---

[*] Most 'blame' the Greek, but there are signs that the change was less abrupt, more gradual and more widespread.

[†] [Dre92]

[‡] E.g. when the IT that provides robustness itself, such as a clustering or fall-back setup, fails. E.g., in a (sponsored) survey, the Ponemon Institute found that even in 2013, the biggest cause in data center failures was a failure of the uninterruptable power supply (UPS), a system to prevent outages in the first place. I recall this 90's study from Canada, which showed that the number of UPS-failures actually *exceeded* the number of actual util-

In combination with the underlying belief that IT is essentially simple, not complex, this leads to an often seen attitude towards IT: internal IT departments are often seen as low quality, and there sometimes is a utopian belief in the quality of external parties. Of course, very mediocre internal IT departments exist, and there are very good providers of certain services, but there is this bias.

All of this strengthens the low status that IT already has. And this low status has two effects that are interesting for this analysis. The first is that, since IT's status is so low, its *requirements* have a low status too. Business does not take the requirements of IT itself very seriously. It needs to 'provide', not 'require', it is 'supply' not 'demand'. A good example is a product selection process. The business selects products to use, but the requirements are very much directed towards the business functionality, with questions such as "can it handle this subject?" or "can it support that procedure?". Assessments about the quality of the IT side of the product, such as "how does it integrate with the rest of the environment?" or "what is the quality of the internals of the product?"* seldom play a large role in the selection process. Whereas the end-user's requirements are seen as a positive thing (functionality), IT's requirements are seen as limitations on what IT is supposed to be able to provide†. The use of the phrase 'non-functional requirements' for these requirements

---

ity power failures it was meant to cover, but I haven't been able to locate it again.

* This is not by definition completely hidden for a good architect. By asking questions to the product provider about how the product behaves, a good architect can often draw useful conclusions about the inside.

† Namely: everything. Which is obviously unrealistic.

is a sign of this problem. As long as IT is not seen as integral part of the function of an organization, its requirements will remain 'non-functionals'[*].

So, IT is left with the situation that it cannot really put its own requirements as first class citizens on the decision table. This lack of attention for IT's own needs is a driver for IT to put its requirements as architecture *principles* into the process. This is, as we have seen, of course a less than ideal solution, but it is often the only way it can push its own agenda as part of the organization.

A second effect of IT's low status is that it suffers a constant brain drain. Low status leads to lower salaries, which leads to a pressure on the smartest people to move away from IT into more business-oriented functions. In some ways, the shift of 'enterprise architecture' from being about IT towards being about the business reflects this; it is in part an attempt to escape from the low status of the most important (and original) subject (IT complexity[†]) into the high status of the primary business.

All of this will only change if organizations become deeply aware of the fact that IT is not simple, and that difficulties in IT are not *just* a matter of poor performance of the IT people.

A concept that is inherently inconsistent anyway. Every requirement that is mentioned can only have a meaning if it is connected to use (Wittgenstein, again). Performance, security, backups, maintenance, all of these only have meaning because there are use cases in the organization where these are in play, some, such as performance for instance, have even a clear 'functional' meaning for the end users of that performance.

Business environments have become more complex too, e.g., due to increased regulatory demands and product innovations. But a major difference between business and IT is that businesses are still largely driven by human behavior and humans can compensate where IT systems cannot.

Of course IT can often perform better, there is a lot of junk and unnecessary complexity being created. There is much to be gained still in many IT operations. IT is not blameless by definition, on the contrary. But the way businesses often ignore complexity as a fundamental aspect of the terrain makes matters much worse. Many difficulties simply result from the enormous unavoidable complexity inherent in the field*.

Larger organizations often have a 'Lead Legal Counsel'. Laws and regulations also have some of the complexity of enterprise architecture (a lot of complexity, more interpretation and fuzziness, slightly less interconnectedness†) and everybody agrees that one needs such a function that specializes in it to be able to handle legal matters. The legal field also moves slowly, laws and regulations take years to come to fruition and be implemented‡. Organizations accept this

---

* And 'silver bullets' like cloud computing are not going to make that go away, they probably will only make it more complex as they produce demand-supply bottlenecks in the middle of your enterprise architecture, making it difficult to manage your landscape holistically. See appendix A for some notes on cloud computing.

† One could argue that the complexity of the legal area is part of the complexity of the enterprise and hence the subject matter for enterprise architecture is *by definition* the sum of all complexities of the entire organization. It is the work of enterprise architecture to find the *relevant* complexities in all parts of the enterprise and it thus has to take all of them into the consideration. Hence, from a complexity perspective, most organizations these days probably need enterprise architecture specialists long before they need legal specialists. This is also another good example to show that *collaboration* is a *conditio sine qua non*.

‡ Which is, I have to repeat, not that different from IT. From the first ideas about software defined infrastructure, for instance, to widespread availability and use will also take many years.

from the legal field, they are acutely aware of the risks they run when they ignore the legal specialists. Organizations are not yet often visibly aware of the risks they run if they ignore the enterprise architects, who are also less recognizable as specialists because they are not so much subject matter specialists but enterprise-spanning complexity specialists*.

Summarizing

Enterprise architecture is 'marooned between the perfect logic of digital systems and the roughness of human imperfection' (see page 69). Enterprise architecture is like *The Chess Game from Hell*. We humans with our 'skulls of limited size' (Dijkstra) are out of our depth trying to fully master it. Our answer to that frustration is a flight into a make-believe world where complex reality is replaced with simple models, simple targets and simple rules. This does not work as well as intended and thirty years of trying to make it work has amply shown this. If we are not harsh, we could say that current methods are not all bad, but that they may be like a five-year old playing chess, while we need to operate on the level of a chess master to be able to get the results that we need. So, the question is, what should we do?

Really good enterprise architects are partly also scarce because they are not so much subject-matter specialists, i.e. specialist in a *subject*, such as enterprise architecture frameworks like TOGAF or FEAF, but specialists in handling multi-subject complexity issues *in collaboration with* the real subject-matter specialists.

The secret of good architecture is having
more than meets the eye
Annabelle Selldorf

5 Playing 'Enterprise Chess'

NOW THAT WE have established how difficult enterprise architecture really is, and what we are up against, we can turn to possible solutions for our problems. Sumarizing, the problems we face when trying to make enterprise architecture work are:

- The real complexity of the Business-IT landscape is where enterprise architecture must have an effect, but that real complexity is way beyond the capability of a human to grasp;
- Enterprise architecture must function in an environment that is unknowable in full and unpredictable to boot;
- Human beings, when 'threatened' by these unsurmountable problems, tend to react with the (biologically built-in) 'freeze' or 'flight' — fleeing into make-believe worlds with simple rules and simple models — or reaction, instead of mustering the necessary 'fight' reaction. But . . .
- Simplistic solutions like principles and guidelines and abstract future states have too little effect on the real problem, and carry significant risks;
- The belief in the effectiveness of logical rules is strengthened by our culture, which places classical logical arguments at the root of what it is to be intelligent.

When we want to create a working enterprise architecture setup, we are therefore up against a very complex problem *and* biological/psychological and cultural hurdles. Actually, the biological/psychological hurdle falls away when we are able to present a convincing way to handle all that complexity. After all, the flight into oversimplified solutions comes from the stress of feeling that we are unable to do what we think we must. So, the question becomes: how do we handle complexity and unpredictability in enterprise architecture? That may sound as an impossible task, but frankly, as history has shown, humans are often able to overcome complexity, as they can fight complexity with a complexity of their own: *collaboration*.

Collaboration

While we are up against enormous complexity in enterprise architecture, and vagueness and contradiction to boot, we tend to forget that we also have an army at our hand: the employees of the organization. Because, while it is true that no single person in the organization can know enough to make the right decisions, the know how *is* there. The problem is that all the know how is spread across the organization. Those business analysts in accounting know everything that one needs to know about the accounting domain. The domain leads over at reporting know all the nooks and crannies of reporting. In fact, all over the organization, there is knowledge at the level of detail that we need. What we therefore need to set up is *effective collaboration*.

The first requirement for setting up that collaboration is to keep in mind at all times that we need to organize the *real* know how, embodied in certain employees.

Let's illustrate with an example. Suppose we have a hospital. In a simplified description, the hospital consists of resources such as machinery, operating rooms, beds, et cetera, and a staff. For simplicity sake, let's say the staff consists of doctors and hospital management. Doctors have studied medicine, hospital management has studied health management. To get good medical care, above all we need good doctors to treat the patients.

Now, suppose our hospital is a bad hospital, that is, it is not as good as other hospitals in curing patients. It might be that all the resources are there and that all the doctors are really good. In that case, it is a matter of organizing better. But if the doctors are bad, no amount of extra 'health management professionals' is going to turn this bad hospital into a good hospital. Patients need a good doctor first and above all. More 'health management' will not turn bad doctors into good ones. This is like projects in IT: no amount of brilliant project management is going to make a project that is executed by poor designers and engineers into a successful project. Where a project with brilliant designers and engineers and bad project management has a chance of success, a project with bad designers and engineers and very good project management will almost certainly fail[*].

The same is true in enterprise architecture. In our setup we must not forget that the first and foremost thing to do is to organize enterprise architecture so the best 'architects' make the design decisions. They need not be called '(enterprise)

As the project mentioned in chapter 1 illustrated. All the attention of the executives went into project management, almost none into architecture. The result was a waste of 150 million euro of public funds.

architects' of course. Sometimes they are called 'business analysts' or 'domain leads'; they come in many guises. But they are the people who know their domain *and* are able to decide on what is a good design decision, both for IT and for the business, for that domain; 'good' being somewhat difficult to pin down, obviously, just as a good move in chess is hard to pin down in a simple and clear description.

The question then becomes more one of organization. What we need is to set up our enterprise architecture function so all this know how can be effectively be brought to the table. What we need is a well-designed enterprise architecture *governance*, such that all this fragmented knowledge starts to act as 'one': we need to build our own virtual 'enterprise chess' grand master out of all the know how that is available. This 'virtual grand master' is the one we'll employ to 'define good moves' for the organization.

The basic structure of the 'enterprise chess' setup of enterprise architecture is shown in figure 5.1 on page 99.

Instead of an enterprise architecture function that sits *above* all the design, or one that sits on top *and* between all the design decisions (the 'bottleneck'), we need an enterprise architecture function that enables the 'virtual enterprise chess master' to function. It sits for a large part *below* the actual design process, supporting it with methods and techniques, an administration such as a well kept model of the current state architecture of the organization, and so forth.

Positioning of the enterprise architecture function

Enterprise architecture, as a function, represents a set of overall goals of the organization as a whole, as described

99

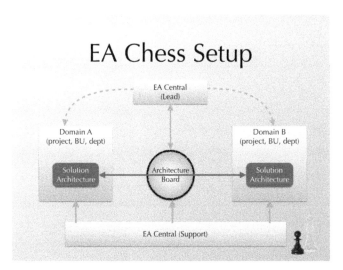

Figure 5.1 The 'enterprise chess' setup

on page 35. These goals naturally reside at the level of the board of an organization.

As illustrated In figure 5.2 on page 100, if we represent the organization as a collection of 'mandates' (e.g. Chief Operating Officer (COO), Chief Client Officer (CCO), Chief Finance Officer (CFO), et cetera, that together form a Board of Directors (BoD) that is being presided by a Chief Enterprise Officer (CEO), then each of these mandates has responsibility for a part of the organization.*†

This exact choice of describing the organization is not important, any other description based on responsibilities will work as well.

In our terminology, such mandates would be natural candidates for high-level domains of the organization.

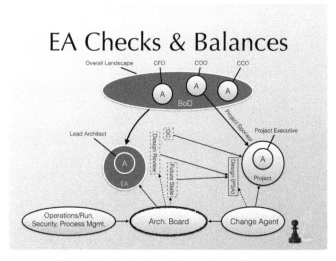

Figure 5.2 Positioning of Enterprise Architecture

As you can see in that figure, there are several example mandates in the Board of Directors in this example (the 'A' denoting 'accountable') . For one of these, the COO, an example project is shown. The COO sponsors this project. The project in question also has a 'Project Executive'*, who is accountable for that project. The project has a design (the Project (Start) Architecture, or PSA) that is the responsibility of the project (and thus for which the Project Executive is accountable†). As argued before, it is important that the *project* is responsible for its own design, otherwise, we get multiple captains on that ship, with all the problems

---

* Cf. PRINCE2, other terminologies for other project management methods apply equally well.
† And the Project Architect responsible.

that brings. From an enterprise architecture perspective the question becomes how enterprise architecture as a function influences that design[*], which is answered below.

The entire Board of Directors (under chairmanship of the CEO) is responsible for the 'Overall Landscape' of the organization[†]. For this overall landscape the goals of enterprise architecture are set by the board[‡]. Just as with a project, this goal must have sponsorship (in this case form the entire board) and someone accountable (in this case the Lead Enterprise Architect). The Lead Enterprise Architect must therefore for enterprise architecture be what the Project Executive is for a project. Together they are the accountable persons for the checks and balances between the specific goal in a domain (project) and the overall landscape goal of enterprise architecture (enterprise).

Domains not feeling responsible for the overall goals of enterprise architecture, was mentioned in chapter 3 as one of the problems with current 'best practice' approaches. But if the entire board feels visibly[29] responsible for the overall landscape goals, it makes domains more readily feel (partly) responsible for the overall landscape, thus fostering cooperation. Minimally, enterprise architecture (as a stakeholder) represents the overall landscape, and together with domain stakeholders it sometimes needs to manage an inescapable conflict of interest between enterprise architecture as the stakeholder for 'the overall landscape' and a domain, such

---

Which in 'enterprise chess' terms is a 'move'.

It is very important that the Lead Enterprise Architect is able to make the board of a company feel responsible for enterprise architecture. If this does not happen, you run into a major obstacle, as described in chapter 7

E.g., via the Future State Architecture — see chapter 6

as a project or a department. But on the longer run, this can
mature into a collaborative feeling of shared ownership of
the 'overall landscape' and 'domain' goals.

Enterprise architecture, as a function, has a number of
specific deliverables it must produce:

Current State Architecture First, it must maintain a reliable documentation of the current Business-IT landscape
of the organization. Maintaining such a documentation
improves the knowledge of the 'start position' for every
'move'. As we noticed in chapter 4, compared with chess
— where the start position for every move is perfectly
known — 'enterprise chess' works with imperfect knowledge of the start position for every move. But the fact
that the knowledge is imperfect does not mean we cannot
improve on it. Improving knowledge of the start position
greatly improves the 'move making' process. More about
what is required to get an adequate documentation of your
current state architecture (or CSA) and how to approach
this can be found in appendix B.

Future State Architecture Second, it must provide a 'future
state architecture'. This future state architecture is guidance for projects, and together with the various demands
(from the business, from maintenance, from IT, et cetera)
form the set of requirements for each change or project.
More on the future state architecture (or FSA) in chapter 6
and a template can be found in appendix C.

Reviews Thirdly, it must produce *reviews* on project architectures and other architectural proposals based on
its responsibility for the 'overall landscape' goals, thus
providing the checks and balances vis-à-vis the change
initiatives. By keeping the projects responsible for their

design and the enterprise architecture function responsible not for the *design* but for the design *review*, both goals are represented in the design process. In the figure on page 100 the enterprise architecture function is also responsible for Quality Control (QC), the review that is not so much on the design decisions taken, but the way the design decisions are created (methodology). Not shown in the figure is the role of the 'current state architecture', which was shortly described above.

Creating reviews is the most important activity of enterprise architecture as it is the only one that *directly* influences the development of the landscape*. All the others are indirect. If you get all the others right, and this one wrong, you lose almost all the potential benefits of enterprise architecture.

Note that in the 'enterprise chess' approach of enterprise architecture, reviewing is not an isolated activity of the enterprise architecture unit. The enterprise architecture unit is responsible, but it is a cooperative activity that stretches across the enterprise. Also important, the design and review activities of project and enterprise architecture respectively need not to be strictly separated in time. It is efficient and effective to have a lot of communication before the actual review.

Standards and guidelines   There is a role for standards and guidelines. The most important ones are the ones that

One could say that the orthodox approach that works with a future state and a small set of foundational principles can be caricatured as 'think small, act big' (try to create the effect on the floor by grand/simple designs and generic rules), while the 'enterprise chess' approach can be caricatured as 'think big, act small' (try to create the big effect on the landscape by acting at the actual change level).

govern *the way the organization performs its architecture work*. E.g., guidelines for project architectures (an example can be found in appendix D), standards for architectural work (such as the modeling language and patterns to use), et cetera.

It is important above all to recognize the goals of enterprise architecture as separate and clearly managed objectives of the organization in their own right. Enterprise architecture must not be something that is delegated to a, rather powerless, central department, it must be clear to a Board of Directors that *they* own the goals of enterprise architecture.*
Because enterprise architecture represents overall goals for the organization, a lack of clear ownership of the goals by the board — just as a COO is accountable for Operations, and a CFO is accountable for Finance — makes it very difficult in every day operations for enterprise architecture to succeed. The board member responsible for day-to-day operations of enterprise architecture should be the Chief Information Officer (CIO) or, if this mandate is not available in the board, the CEO. It should not be one of the other board members, because this kills the checks and balances between that board member's own mandate and the organization-wide 'overall landscape' goals.†

It is also important that the enterprise architecture function doesn't just play 'policeman'. Though the separate 'stakeholdership' for the organization-wide enterprise architecture

---

* Here, often, lies a problem for enterprise architecture, more about that in chapter 7.
† In which case the short term demands of the project generally win from the long term requirements, i.e. enterprise architecture.

goals is essential for it to function, the results in the end come from *collaborating* between the representatives of the various stakeholders. Hence, while a formal product of enterprise architecture is 'review', the most productive setup makes sure that before that review takes place, there is close collaboration and a helpful attitude across the board. Without that, every difference of opinion leads to conflict. With close cooperation*, only the most important issues end up in the most costly and time-consuming decision process (i.e. handling a conflict).

The advantages of a clear setup of responsibilities come to light when goals conflict (as they always will). When a project's goals leads it to propose a certain solution, whereas the overall landscape goals leads to a different solution, there is not so much an architectural conflict but a conflict between organizational goals that come to light in the architectural discussion. Such conflicts will happen on a regular basis and are not a bad thing, but a good thing (and should be seen as such), because they give us the opportunity to fix conflicts stemming from our companies' complex, often imprecise, and sometimes contradictory, goals before they become too damaging.

If a conflict on design decisions occurs, the first thing that should happen is to try to resolve the difference on the work floor (i.e. between the project (or a domain in general) and the central enterprise architecture function). If constructive discussions take place — based on the real

---

Which itself requires transparency in the organization. Something we will return to when we discuss the obstacles for the 'enterprise chess' approach in chapter 7

goals that everybody can recognize and respect — this is what happens most of the time. But sometimes, the difference cannot easily be reconciled. This might be a matter of *opinion** — e.g. the project does not agree with the assessment of enterprise architecture that some solution is risky or leads to problems in the long term — in which case the difference of opinion moves up the 'ladder of escalation'. Moving up the ladder of escalation is costly for both parties, so either one can always opt to give in — not all fights are worth fighting.[†]

But there will always be cases where giving in on either side is not an option. A typical simple example is that for the overall landscape solution A is better, but this takes more time and money than available to the project (at that point a hard limit), which therefore proposes solution B. Solution B, however makes future projects much more problematic and costly. In a case like that, the conflict should rise up the escalation ladder to the board, as it is the board that must decide to either accept the extra cost in the future or the extra cost now.[‡]

---

* Again, this is to be expected. Our setup must not try in vain to prevent all differences of opinion, it must see these as a source of improvement and be able to handle them, or make use of them in a productive manner.

[†] From a pragmatic point of view, I think enterprise architecture has a 'budget' of a few board-level escalations a year, in other cases enterprise architecture may give in and see the 'bad' move as part of the landscape that is not ideal anyway and never will be.

[‡] Or disagree with the assessment of enterprise architecture, of course, and not accept that there will be extra costs in the future. None of these assessments are generally of the 'hard number' type. One of the difficulties is that this subject is always a matter of 'professional estimate' and hard numbers that make a discussion easier are not easy to come by.

Projects and The Architecture Board

Back to our model from page 99. An important question is: what role does the Architecture Board play in that setup?

It is important to stress two things: first it should not be a design office as shown in figure 3.2 on page 56. The Architecture Board should basically be there to *evaluate* designs (including future state guidance of those designs) and thus influence them. You do not want the Architecture Board to be some extra captain on each (project, domain) ship. The second is that the role of the Architecture Board depends on the role of the positioning of the enterprise architecture function itself. In our model, the architecture board is the 'top' of the pyramid of architectural (design) *discussions*, not *decisions*, taking place in the organization, the place where the final discussions and review judgments take place. It is enterprise architecture's equivalent on the overall landscape goals of what a 'project board' is for project goals.

The actual 'judging' discussions on proposed 'enterprise chess moves'* in our landscape thus take place in a *collaboration* of various stakeholders, to be precise: the 'architects' of those domains, called the 'Architecture Board'. Many organizations have such a board. Sometimes these boards are comprised of managers with decision power and the architects are supposed to bring a number of alternatives for that board to decide upon. This is highly ineffective

---

E.g. Project (Start) Architectures.

as it is often only during the *architectural* discussion[*] that various aspects of proposed solutions can come to light. For instance, returning to the example given in chapter 3: if the accounting architect proposes to create certain client reports directly from the accounting system, the reporting architect, who actually knows the aspects of client reporting in much more detail, can ask things like "so, how do you propose that the benchmarks that you need to calculate certain values in your reports are taken into account?". At which point the accounting architect may realize that he did not know these benchmarks were necessary for the reports. A discussion then can ensue, where the reporting architect explains all that is necessary for those reports and what may be needed in the future[†]. The architecture board may find that sourcing these reports directly from the accounting system may have the advantage that it prevents the same numbers to be calculated in different places, but at the cost of adding much data to the accounting environment that is not needed for accounting at all, almost turning that accounting environment to a second data warehouse. It all depends on the details of that discussion to decide[‡] which move is best, but having the right people, or maybe better: the right knowledge, at the table makes these discussions a lot higher in quality and better, more robust decisions are the result. If actual enterprise architecture design choices are made by non-architect

---

[*] Thus amongst *architects*. The setup with management deciding on the basis of proposals by architects is like letting hospital management decide on treatment based on scenarios presented by the doctors.

[†] Or the problem is relegated to a future meeting and both architects are given the task to collaborate on a solution.

[‡] A more appropriate term is probably 'estimate'.

managers on the basis of input of the architects, the managers are in fact playing the role of architects.

Of course, as stated above, discussion should not be limited to reviews in the architecture board. The more collaboration there is in the process *before* that review, the more efficient and effective the process becomes. For project architectures, we can generally keep to a three-stage process:

Phase 1: Before the project architecture (or any other large design, such as a 'target state' for a domain) is in its first official draft, informal cooperation between the project (architect) and other stakeholders (such as enterprise architecture and other domains) takes place.*

Phase 2: When the project architect decides the draft is finished, it is presented to the architecture board for *informal review*. Here the project architecture is discussed as if it was a final proposal for a 'enterprise chess move'. But the idea of this phase is to enable the architecture board members to voice their questions and critiques. The project architect can answer the questions and critiques and at the end has a number of areas where he or she needs to pay extra attention. Depending on the quality of the draft and how much criticism there is, this stage may take place several times.

Phase 3: When the project architect has taken all the feedback under consideration, he creates a final project architecture and offers this for *formal review*. Now, the same happens as in the previous stage, however, the discussion concentrates on what the architecture board members

---

If this does not take place, e.g., because of the 'siege mentality' obstacle described in chapter 7, the process may turn into an unproductive fight between more or less 'complete' solution designs.

consider to be 'no go', design decisions that really should not remain as is, because of the issues they bring for the organization as a whole. At the end of this phase, enterprise architecture publishes a *formal review*. In this review, any 'no go' issues are clearly marked. Any review that contains 'no go' issues is considered to have approval withheld by enterprise architecture.

It is important to note that the review is not a review by the architecture *board*, but it is a review by the enterprise architecture function *based on the input of the architecture board*. This is an important distinction. It gives the enterprise architecture function actual responsibility for its side of the checks and balances. The Lead Enterprise Architect must be accountable for the review. Again, this is quite like the position of the Project Executive of a project in a mature project management method like PRINCE2. There, the project board may contain e.g. a *Senior User* and a *Senior Supplier*, the decisions are formally those of the Project Executive. It is not as if the project board comes to a democratic vote*. That does not mean that a project board, or an architecture board for that matter, should not operate on the basis of *consensus*. Like a good Project Executive, a good Lead Enterprise Architect constantly strives for consensus, but has the final say — for instance, when the architecture board cannot come to a consensus opinion†. In practice, amongst good architects

---

* Or at least not in a mature project management method such as PRINCE2.
† There are a few reasons why the Lead Enterprise Architect needs this position. One is to prevent possible horse trading between domains. Another is as a prevention against the 'siege mentality' mentioned in chapter 7

(that are not burdened by 'political' targets) the consensus happens more often than not[*].

Who needs to be in that Architecture Board? Those that bring important 'domain' knowledge to the table:

The Lead Enterprise Architect   The Lead Enterprise Architect chairs the board and is responsible for producing the results. More about these results and their role in the enterprise later. Again, the Lead Enterprise Architect must be like the Project Executive in the PRINCE2 project management method. He is a delegated owner of the organization's enterprise architecture goals. The Lead Enterprise Architect will normally be supported by one or two members of the enterprise architecture function (some of his team members).

Business/IT know how from each major domain   The Architecture Board discusses what are the best 'enterprise chess moves' (design decisions) for the organization. You need to have know how of the domains, both at a business level and at an IT level[*▸]. Sometimes, these may be rolled into one, sometimes you need two persons. The less persons you need, the better it works. Sometimes you may use one person for multiple domains, for instance if that person is part of a 'change' department that serves multiple

---

'Great' minds think alike... On the other hand, between architects with deep-running differences of opinion (such as on the effectiveness of using a principle-based enterprise architecture approach) consensus remains a problem.

domains. Above all, these participants need to have good design skills.

'Run' and Infrastructure know how   Moves in the landscape must not only work for the business, the direct 'users' of IT solutions. They must also work for the people who keep the machinery running. This is often forgotten, but you better find out that your solution cannot be reliably backed up before you go into production…

Security & Risk Officer   Security & Risk is best handled at the design stage of a project. Bolting security on when all is said and done generally does not work.[30]

Process Management   Often, an organization has a team that works with documenting and understanding the entire process landscape of the business. These people are invaluable to check if no processes are forgotten, that they are completely in focus, and so forth.

Not all of these have the same impact at every discussion, so you can be flexible in who is attending. But you need a bit of a fixed body of people that collectively have the know how. If you have different people attending all the time, you will have a lot of repeat discussions and that is very tiresome for those that always attend. It is also a good idea to have the project architects of large projects attend architecture board discussions. This may lead to an overly large and unwieldy architecture board if there is no overlap between project architects on the one hand and domain architects on the other, in which case you need to find a

---

[*] Note that if you are doing enterprise architecture for the IT business unit, the 'business' we are talking about here is the business of IT: the IT business unit's functions and processes.

good pragmatic solution to make sure project architects are part of the discussion.

During the project, design choices are made that are either not covered by the approved project architecture or are different from what is in the project architecture. It is a good idea to have a final review by the enterprise architecture unit before the result is accepted for production. But when at that moment large differences are discovered, it is often too late to do anything about it. Organizational pressure will win out for the short term. Hence, it is wise to have as part of your enterprise architecture governance to have regular updates by the project architects, where they have to report any additions and/or changes to the project's architecture, on top of the rule that nothing may be realized unless it is covered by the project architecture. This together creates an 'early warning system'.

The enterprise architecture team

You need a few good 'enterprise' architects in your central enterprise architecture team. What you need are people who*:

- are very analytical;
- can handle complexity;
- can model well;
- can learn (new businesses and new technologies) fast;
- are independent and steadfast;
- are not afraid to go against the stream;

Several of these are a matter of coaching the team members, some are a matter of (developed) talent.

- are able to understand the problems of others and act responsibly towards these problems[*];
- are able to estimate the effect of scaling on a design decision such as model patterns;
- are able to 'feel' where the relevant details are;
- are able to find the root cause of IT problems quickly[†];
- are able to explain complicated issues very clearly[‡].
- are charming[**].

In short: they must be 'enterprise chess' masters. Now, it is clear that you will not find all capabilities in all your team members. Here again, the way forward is to create a *collaborative* team that covers all of these capabilities. But all of your team members must have all of these skills at some minimal level.[31]

Given the low status of IT in many organizations, still, not many organizations are aware that they are in fact in a fight for very, very rare talents if they want to have effective enterprise architecture. It still happens that functions such

---

[*] They do not actually *own* the problems, but they should act in such a way that all the stakeholders are taken seriously, so a type of behavior that mimics ownership.

[†] Good design is meant to prevent root causes. The ability to find root causes of problems quickly is the other side of the 'design skills' coin. They develop strongest when in lockstep.

[‡] Being able to explain matters clearly is both a sign of communication skills as well as a sign of deep understanding.

[**] This sounds weird, but enterprise architects always function on the edge of the checks & balances between local and global, as well as between short term and long term, requirements that make up the field. They will often have a message that people do not want or like to hear, in which they have to be independent and steadfast. Having charm is therefore an important asset.

as enterprise architecture are filled with people who needed some function because their old job was gone, or they were not able to keep up. This happens up to the highest level in organizations. I once heard, for instance, that two companies merged and there was only one 'Company Controller' function available in the merged company. One of the controllers of the merging companies got that job. The other was made CIO. Organizations are often still not quite certain what to think of IT and IT-related functions and sometimes still seem to think that IT (and enterprise architecture) is in essence simple and that anybody can do it*.

So, where do you find good enterprise architects? In my experience, the best candidates:

- have a strong background in complex engineering, preferably application architecture, which is still the most complex domain[†] in IT and the best training ground for prospective enterprise architects;
- have sufficient experience. In our field, you are not done learning when you finish your tertiary education. Our field is like the medical field, where a decent period of real-world experience is needed to turn those fresh from medical school into good doctors who are

---

As mentioned before; enterprise architects presenting simplified make-believe worlds to management without convincing management of the actual complexity that is hidden behind those simple messages work against their own needs.

Though infrastructure architecture has been growing in complexity and with the advent of software defined this and that, and can thus be considered the equal to application architecture in complexity.

able to make the right diagnosis and select the best treatment most of the time;

Finally, you need not only build a team, you need to keep it alive. One pattern, seen pretty often in organizations is that the best and brightest in some domain are selected for a special department. E.g., the best software engineers are selected to form the 'software engineering methodology' department. Or they become the 'software architecture team'. This works, initially, but a few years later they tend to lag more and more. They become bureaucratic (e.g., as development environment maintainers), or overly academic. The reason for this is simple: *Use it or lose it*. Unless you keep your skills alive, they die. A skill is something that needs constant activity, because it is know 'how' and not know 'what'.

The same is true for the central enterprise architecture team. The team members must remain active in projects*, as project architects or supporting project architects. If they do not, their knowledge of both organization and technology becomes ultimately shallow. In my experience, skills of architects that are not kept alive become stale in a period of two to three years. My personal estimate is that central enterprise architects need to spend roughly fifty percent of their time in real projects. So, you need roughly a team

---

* Another option is to make sure they are still active in technology some-where, e.g. privately. If you are an enterprise architect, you need to re-main active in complex design problems in some way, or your complexity-handling skills will starve. Even the Lead Enterprise Architect must find a minimal amount of complex technical work to keep his estimation capa-bility alive.

twice the size of the central work, otherwise you will 'use the people up'.

If the central enterprise architects also work in projects (which is necessary to keep them skilled), you need to make sure you handle separation of duties well. Generally, when one of the central team's architects works for another domain, that domain is in charge of his design. His position must not be other than any other domain architect. His or her designs follow the same governance, undergo the same reviews, and so forth. If 'central' architects are active in a project, the lead architect should be very happy if they challenge existing guidance from enterprise architecture. It means that the collaborative structure which is meant to fight complexity — with its clear representation of the 'opposing' sides of the enterprise architecture checks and balances — is actually working. But you can imagine that it is not easy on people to have this kind of independence and it requires mature and trustworthy management on all sides.

Principles and guidelines

If principles and guidelines are generally not effective to produce enterprise architecture's results, should we abandon them? The answer is no, they remain useful in several ways. It is the *enforcing* of principles and guidelines as a *design* method *instead* of making collaborative design choices that is dangerous. Using principles and guidelines as *prescriptive* rules is what is risky. Using guidelines as *descriptive* rules for the organization can be useful, however. But we should drop the term '(design) *principle*' in most cases. Good design cannot be delivered by following simple rules, that was not true for the utopian architects of the physical (like Le Corbusier) of half a century ago* and it is likewise not true for enterprise architecture today. Elevating a basic design decision — because that is what it is — to a principle stifles discussion and thought that is necessary for good answers to complex questions. The organization is not that simple that a few simple basic rules can give you the answer. The designers in your organization, those that design the 'enterprise chess' moves, must have these guidelines in their system. The master chess player knows that material advantage is often a good thing. It is part of his system. He does not need to have that one explicitly as a rule to check, each time he looks for an alternative. There are far too many 'rules' for this to work out. The architect of the physical knows that a house needs to have enough daylight in the interior[†]. The same is true in enterprise architecture. *The rules must be 'in' the architect, not the other way around.* The rules will be part of each 'design decision' because the architects will have them in their system. This is why you need architects that have all these basic capabilities and that experience mentioned above. You need good enterprise architects much more than you need good enterprise architecture principles.

But guidelines can be useful for non-architects as a sort of basic idea. If the project manager is aware that there

---

[*] See page 61.

[†] A typical narrow vision from western architects that discussed the principles that ended up in Le Corbusier's Athen's Charter. They all came from affluent temperate climate zones. But a lot of daylight might be a problem in the Saharan desert climate, for instance and there, a cool house might be more important than a light house.

are certain guidelines, he may be prevented to try to go all over the place with his project. It must, however, be crystal clear for each project manager that 'comply or explain' is not practiced and that there is a more intelligent process needed to come to the right design decisions.

Secondly, guidelines can also be useful for educational and communicative purposes. Just as I can teach my son the first tactical insights for the game of chess in the form of the first simple rules, central enterprise architecture can teach the organization a couple of guidelines. But just as with my son, these guidelines will always come with a warning: just following them is not going to get you your results. Following them is acceptable for early beginners in chess and it is likewise acceptable for amateur enterprise architects, which is not what we aspire to be.

And finally, there are rules that are indeed there never to be broken. I would not call these 'design principles' but they are almost like the rules of the game. In chess, for instance, the rule is that if you touch one of your pieces, you must move it* and if you move a piece and you let go, it has moved and you're not allowed to change the move anymore. These are rules of the game that are taken seriously when playing official matches, but when you play a game with your child and the child makes an error, you can of course allow the child to go back and try again. So, these rules about moving are part of chess game rules, but you can imagine that you will not follow them in certain situations and you still can call that 'playing chess'*▸.

Unless you say at the same time "J'adoube", which is French for "I'm setting (this piece) straight".

In Enterprise Architecture there are also rules like that. Take for instance the use of separate infrastructure setups for Development, Testing, Acceptance and Production (DTAP). Because of what they are meant for, but also for compliance, security and so forth, there are many rules governing the use of these environments. You should not develop in the Production environment, it is far too risky. Having the Production environment depend on the running of the Development (or Test or Acceptance) environment is also not a good idea, because that amounts to the same problem. Data in the company is also governed by rules and regulations, and even law. This means all kinds of requirements are there for your Production environment. But in Development, such rules can be counterproductive. E.g., security standards are high in Production, whereas they are much lower in Development. So, a very good rule is that Development, Test, Acceptance and Production environments should be separated: they should be *completely* unable to influence each other.

Now, suppose some system is a system where constantly new algorithms for, say, risk calculations are developed by risk researchers, then developed, tested and put into use by risk managers. The designer of that setup may well say: "All these environments must be equal. Let's make sure by letting the Test, Acceptance and Production environment use the stored infrastructure settings of the Development environment directly." Such a design choice breaks the rule of separation of those environments and should be forbidden.

---

*◄ We're getting dangerously close to Wittgenstein's 'family resemblances' here. . .

It is quite sensible to write such hard rules down and enforce them. As you never know how much of a 'hacker' your designer is, you cannot trust the assumption that no one will ever do something as stupid as that. So, a rule like that, a rule founded in very strong, unwielding requirements, may be set as a 'not to be broken' rule for the designers. It is a 'never to be ignored' requirement. If you like, you can call it a principle.[32]

As we noticed in the previous chapter, principles are sometimes pushed by IT because they form the only way for IT to get its own requirements recognized by the business. But it is a poor mechanism, you are setting your internal relation between business and IT into a sort of conflict mode. Many principles I have seen in organizations are in fact (hidden) requirements by the IT side of the business. The best solution is to take these requirements seriously as part of the business requirement process, instead of establishing as a breaking mechanism against the business' innovative drive. IT is an integral part of doing business and the role of IT's own requirements should reflect that. Doing enterprise architecture means that you need to look at the whole of the Business-IT landscape*.

Ironically, the enterprise architects that argue most vehemently that enterprise architecture is 'not about IT' (but about the business) damage one of the most important aspects of enterprise architecture: the holistic approach. Enterprise architecture means that you need to see IT as an integral part of doing business, a first class citizen.

Product selections

In the previous chapter, we highlighted the problem of 'canned architecture', the architecture that you do not create yourself, but that you get when you buy some product or platform to use in your organization's landscape.

In the worst case, the business buys a product and then leaves it to IT to figure out how to keep the landscape in good order[*]. In the best case, enterprise architecture is part of the product selection process, judging the canned architecture for its effect on the overall landscape before the product is bought.

Such a judgment may sound impossible because vendors are seldom open about their architecture, it is after all a part of their competitive edge. But the internals of a canned architecture is not by definition completely hidden for a good architect. By asking questions to the product provider about how the product behaves technically, by visiting peers that use the product[†], a good architect can often draw useful conclusions. For instance, when the documentation of the core product of a company that started out in the

---

[*] This 'worst case' is actually 'common practice'.

[†] The peers you visit are often selected by the product's provider. This is a bit of a problem, but you can still get useful information if you ask the right questions. One thing I have found to be very useful: if the provider is not willing to give you two years worth of release notes of product updates in the first place (I always ask for this), a peer may grant you access to them. Release notes are extremely valuable for judging the robustness of a product. E.g., release notes can tell you how long certain problems linger in a product or if they return after formally having been fixed.

late eighties of the previous century mentions C++*, and —
when asked about an XML interface instead of the mentioned
CSV interface — the sales person says that this is possible but
accidentally drops that the XML is first translated to CSV, the
architect can deduce that the core of the product is probably
old and that the provider is weary to change the core† and
instead only tries to adapt its outer layer. That leads to the
conclusion that there is a substantial risk that the provider
will have to do a major overhaul of the core of its product
in the years to come, and the enterprise architect asks the
business: do you really want to be the guinea pig in that
process? Because that is not a technical issue, that is a
business issue. Suppose one of the provider's competitors
has just finished such an overhaul process and has rebuilt
and modernized its product in a major new release? You can
expect that that architecture is more stable in the years to
come. Is that a more attractive proposal for the business?

Product vendors have their own architecture that they are
selling you. One thing to watch out for is that they often also
sell you what they consider 'best practice' for implementation
of the product in your landscape. This is a slippery subject.
While the vendor generally knows his product well and
can indeed say what is best from the product's view, that
is not necessarily best from your organization's view. Your
business stakeholders often want that IT follows 'vendor best
practices' (sometimes even writing that down as a 'principle',

---

As everywhere in this book: do not worry if you have no idea what the
technical terms exactly stand for. The argument does not depend on them.
This is an understatement. Sometimes this is the external effect of undocu-
mented code that the provider doesn't even understand himself anymore.

with all the dangers that brings), but what they should do is create a best fit with their own landscape of which they should feel themselves to be the owner*. You do not get a good landscape by following the independent (and often conflicting) 'best practices' of each vendor. You get a mess.

In fact, a vendor selling you a product that needs to integrate with the rest of your architecture may have a best practice that above all caters to the best interests of the vendor himself. E.g. if the product can connect to your landscape with both flat files readily created in the format that some of your other systems can handle as import, that may sound attractive. But that import mechanism of the system that you already use may be restricted† and not be your best choice. The mechanism proposed by the vendor also has the effect that the vendor's support load becomes much lighter: they have just the correctness of their output file to consider. If it is good, the rest is your problem. Another integration method may have a higher support load for the vendor. From their perspective, you choosing the archaic solution may be 'best practice', it leads to the least number of problems seen *at their end*. One should never forget: in the end the provider looks out for himself before looking out for you. Looking out for you is important in the long term, certainly, but it remains secondary by definition.

---

* With enterprise architecture helping them to own it in a professional way.
† E.g., the import restricted may be able to import thousands of records but not be able to report *which* record was the problem when the import failed to load completely; it can only report *that* it failed somewhere.

Outsourcing & Supply/Demand

As enterprise architecture is about the coherence and future of the entire Business-IT landscape, it is important to understand the effects of outsourcing. Generally, what outsourcing does is make a separation in the landscape. This can be a separation in technology (e.g., outsourcing your data center, cloud-based* solutions) or it can be outsourcing in governance (e.g., outsourcing development of which the result becomes part of your landscape, outsourcing the staffing of your data center to a separate provider). Whatever the type of outsourcing, the separation has an effect on enterprise architecture in that it makes it harder to create answers that cross a demand-supply boundary.

It is of course nonsense to say that all outsourcing is bad, but one type of hidden outsourcing is bad for enterprise architecture: running your IT as a business. Running your internal IT as if it was an outsourced business creates a deep rift in your organization between business and IT, a funnel where it is very difficult to get mature and complex decisions through. Running IT as a business has been conventional wisdom for a long time, but as Bob Lewis has written [Lew10], it has many negative effects.

Any form of demand-supply separation forms a bottleneck of sorts. As many firms that outsourced a lot of their IT noticed, there were not only benefits, there was also a cost to pay. Many firms have now started to insource more and more after they experienced the drawbacks.

An underestimated source for new complexity in enterprise architecture landscapes of any but the most simple organizations, see appendix A.

I use a golden rule when thinking about outsourcing: when the size of the *description* of the demand is at least an order of magnitude less than the size of the *description* of the supply, outsourcing is possible. Let me explain. If you want to build a large IT system to support a complex administration, the full description of all the requirements will take up quite a bit of documentation. The requirements are very complex. But the solution does not need to be. But there are also opposite situations. If you want to lease a data line with an exceptionally small bit loss for some reason* the *description* of what you want is very small, but, depending on the numbers, the solution to get this result — and thus its description — might be very large and complex. In IT, that means that outsourcing stuff that can be defined in simple terms is OK, but outsourcing something that is very complex†, is not. And you need to be careful, because it is quite easy to overlook a lot of complexity. You can outsource building your web site to another company, but if that web site needs to be integrated with your back office systems, suddenly the requirements of integration makes everything very complex and to make matters worse, they span a demand-supply boundary. The simple rule is: do not outsource architectural elements with complex requirements,

---

* In the real world this problem is solved by higher level protocols that re-transmit on error.

† Or variable, vague, et cetera. An important aside: this is also true for out-sourcing *development*. For complex projects, it is best to stay in control and use IT providers only as a provider of people, not as a provider of *solutions*. The lack of inside skills often brings organizations to shop for providers that will develop custom-build solutions, but it is a common cause of under-performing projects.

especially with complex requirements with respect to the rest of your landscape.[33]

Agile and Enterprise Architecture

There is something to say for the statement that the approach as proposed in this book is a form of *agile* enterprise architecture. Agile is the name for a software development philosophy that opposes more directed waterfall-like approaches and prefers more situational and evolutionary approaches (small steps, called 'sprints' in an agile-related project methodology like Scrum) to software engineering. Many organizations, especially those in IT, are trying to incorporate aspects of Agile into their operations these days.

Agile is — unsurprisingly — not a silver bullet. It has drawbacks. There is much agreement that Agile does not scale very well, that it more easily leads to chaotic solutions and landscapes and that planning and (cost) control is difficult. Some of this is because of Agile not being executed well, e.g., Agile says for instance that you should solve the most difficult problems first, because basing the first steps on the simple parts easily leads to weak foundations. You can't build a skyscraper on the foundations laid out for a bird watcher cabin. But some of the drawbacks are essential effects of the approach.

An obvious mitigating policy is to strengthen (enterprise) architecture. Enterprise architecture can be the guiding mechanism for agile change initiatives. In fact, the role of enterprise architecture in projects can be the same in both waterfall and agile approaches. As mentioned before, the waterfall approach (design – build – test – deploy) has problems with volatility, which — as we noticed in the previous chapter — is generally large. Waterfall approaches need to revisit their design and planning at every change. If they don't do that, they are running the risk of not delivering what is needed. So, the architecture of a waterfall project needs to be adapted constantly and the result of adaptations must be handled by project management, something mature methods such as PRINCE2 are capable of. A real problem is that this capability is often not used at all. A project that is agile, that changes time, budget and other aspects while reacting in an agile manner to its surroundings, is not what management requires or expects. Management requires *control*: deliver the — initially defined — results within time and budget. It is easy to see that such an attitude does away with the essentially agile nature of project management methods like PRINCE2.

In waterfall projects, much of the design activity is at the start and we only change the design if confronted with important reasons to do so. In agile, we still need to set up an initial design that assures we can end up with a skyscraper, then move forward with the mini-waterfall sprints. So, from the agile perspective, you must make enterprise architecture part of the team, but as we have seen, enterprise architecture cannot be the know-it-all that is required for that role. As a first order solution, one could make the architecture part of the agile project's deliverables, with the rule that everything is 'created' in the architecture (described) before it is created in the real (built). That way, architecture becomes part of the agile process and deliverables. Every time we change (adapt, deepen, extend) the architecture of what the project will deliver, we need to go through the architecture design process.

For agile projects, having a strong, agile and integrated architecture governance is even more important than in waterfall. While steps in agile are mini-waterfalls consisting of design-build-test-deploy activities, the overall design, the architecture, is something that is a continuous process.

Agile methodologies stress the importance of getting usable results for 'end users' quickly. The 'agile coach' often stresses this aspect. I personally think that while each 'move' needs to build towards the end result, each move need not be independently 'usable' by end users. Sometimes, as in chess, you need to make a few moves in concert to get a 'result'. 'Strict agile' therefore comes with the dangers of the *low-hanging fruit* approach to results (see also appendix A, for more on this).

Budget, Time & Scope

If you look at project management as managing the triangle time–budget–result, projects are still often by and large managed on the first two. These are after all tangible and not that complex. Often, *timeboxing* is used as a way to manage these. Timeboxing is a project planning technique that is intended to manage the risk of going over time and budget. The project's schedule is split up in 'time boxes' which may not be exceeded. If what has been planned for a time box cannot be delivered, the scope may be reduced, i.e., we produce less. Of course, what is often first reduced is quality; many quick-and-dirty solutions have been created under time pressure, such as the one coming from timeboxing.

Timeboxing without a strong role for quality management (e.g., the quality management that is also part of enterprise architecture governance) is a recipe for problems in your landscape; project productivity soars, the landscape suffers.

Given that we cannot predict exactly what we are going to run into, given the complexity and unpredictability of the Business–IT landscape, we might want to turn this around. As in chess, sometimes we need to think long and hard about a certain move, sometimes we are on a robust path and we can move more quickly. Forcing the chess player to always think one minute per move — no more, no less — is anathema to the flexibility required. We might want to move to a system where there still is a penalty for using to much time (or budget), but where the requirements of the situation are leading with respect to time and budget needed.

It boils down to this: if you *steer* projects effectively mainly on time and budget, what you *get* is a result defined as time and budget*. The effect of which is that you throw away the prime reason why you are doing the project in the first place: the results it must deliver. Though good agile methods such as DSDM stress the importance of "never compromise quality", in practice, the steering on overall landscape goals and quality is often absent. The short term goals, the immediate use cases, survive the approach, but the wider 'overall landscape' and quality goals suffer.

What is thus required is a more relaxed attitude to time and budget and more of a focus on delivered value. This is really a problem, because the actual value of that extra time

---

* Timeboxing is a very good method to reduce waste in projects. Productivity often soared for IT development project types when it was introduced.

spent is often in details in a complex landscape for which higher management does not have the time or background to go into. This is another reason why a strong position of an independent enterprise architecture function, which acts on behalf of higher management to guard these overall landscape goals, is important.

Now, earlier in this chapter, we have focused primarily on project architectures, as these in practice define the actual 'moves' that build your landscape. And the governance setup we so far described is one of checks & balances, where the project is responsible for its 'goals of limited scope' and the central enterprise architecture role is responsible for 'goals for the landscape as a whole'. But only working via governance on that design document is not an optimal solution. To keep architectural matters flexible, fast and smooth, it is a good idea to make the independent enterprise architecture function a part of project boards as a separately recognized stakeholder*. Time, budget and the direct scope of the project are generally already well represented (executive, users, suppliers). But the users are not good representatives of the 'overall landscape' requirements, and without someone to represent that, it will be close to impossible to keep the effect of independent projects on the overall landscape benign.

It is also a good idea to have the 'run' organization as a stakeholder on board, as well as security, minimally in an 'informed' role, so they can signal possible issues in an early stage, e.g., via the architecture governance processes.

He, who predicts the future, lies,
even if he is telling the truth
Arabic proverb

6 Managing the Future

THERE ARE MANY ways for organizations to come to grips with the future. Large organizations often deploy several of them. Enterprise architecture has generally only employed two: *forecasting* and *backcasting*.

What 'orthodox' enterprise architecture these days normally does is: first define a 'future Business-IT landscape' that is to be worked towards, then look at what is necessary to get the organization there. That mechanism is also known from the domain of business strategy, where it is called *backcasting*. What the enterprise architecture function does is the same, and — as we already noticed in chapter 4 — this generally works as well in enterprise architecture as it does in chess, namely: not.

The enterprise or IT architects are also often given the task to create a 'road map' based on an analysis of developments — often mainly in IT. If the road map is based on a goal, it is backcasting. But if the road map is based on the analysis of expected future development (e.g. technology life cycles) we are basing the road map on an attempt to predict the future; we are *forecasting*. In the somewhat distant past, forecasting was an important task for enterprise architecture; the enterprise architects traveled the world, visiting conferences and trying to find out where IT was heading. These conferences — they still exist — were filled with pundits doing their best to predict the future*▸.

134

These days, sending enterprise architects all over the world to try to predict the future is out of fashion, the results have been meager and organizations have learned their lesson. Some forecasting still exists, mainly in the technology domain (technology 'road maps'), because real value can be had from these. In reality, all kinds of disruptive innovation still happen all the time, as even powerful and large firms like Microsoft, Nokia, RIM* have experienced, who have seen their road maps become obsolete by disruptive innovation by the likes of Apple, Google et cetera.[34]

The backcasting of classic enterprise architecture does not have such a bad name as forecasting. The main reason is that the mechanism at first sight still seems to work, especially because it is 'best practice' to redefine the future state at a regular basis[†], say yearly, and change it with the changes in environment and strategic goals of the organization. Hence, that the sketched future state never comes to pass is seen as an accepted part of working with a 'future state' architecture. And of course, it is seductive[‡]. What people seldom realize that if you build a landscape of elements that have an average life span of fifteen years with a strategy that changes direction every few years, chances are that you end up with a mess.

---

*◄ If you want some fun, reading past predictions is often hilarious. E.g. even in the nineties, when the internet was rapidly gaining a foothold, major pundits and publications still predicted a rapid rise of interactive videotext (a kind of teletext, the French Minitel was the most successful one) until it would be ubiquitous in a few years time.

* Blackberry
† On paper, at least.
‡ See page 85.

Before sketching which better strategic instrument we can bring to the table, the shortcomings of the existing approach will be illustrated with an example.

How things can go pear-shaped

Suppose* we are an asset manager that specializes in taking over complete asset and liability management for pension funds; this is called 'fiduciary management'. We are in the position that our accounting system is at the end of its life cycle and needs to be replaced. We need to select a new system and implement it in our landscape — in other words: define the new landscape or architecture.

Now, our business has a strategy to minimize complexity and risk in our asset management, called 'security and simplicity'. Part of that strategy is that we do not allow investment in derivatives of derivatives (too risky), such as 'swaptions', and we do not accept all kinds of extremely specialized assets such as 'mortality rate swaps' (too specialized). Never mind if you do not know what these asset types are, any field has its specialized products, tools and instruments. Since we are selecting a new accounting system, we have a list of functions the new system must support. We have 'must haves', 'should haves', 'could haves' and 'nice to haves', and these are written down in our request for proposal that we

---

I must stress that this situation is hypothetical and in no way reflects the actual reality of my employer or any of my past employers. This situation reflects something that *could* happen in the situation of a fiduciary manager, not that it *has* happened. We only used it (as I do here) as an example in discussions.

send out to different accounting system vendors. Our list does not have the 'swaption' and the 'mortality rate swap' in its 'must have' or even 'should have' category. After all, what use is having a business strategy if the business itself can ignore it if it wants to?

After a well executed procurement process system *BigAccounts* is selected, and this system cannot do swaptions and it cannot do mortality rate swaps, but that is no problem as we do not need these. The next phase is to design the Business-IT landscape that must be produced by the implementation project. And the question arises: where do we source our formal reports? With the old system, we had to source these from our Data Warehouse as the old system could not handle all the necessary product details. But doing all sorts of calculations in the Data Warehouse is risky, because the same numbers are sometimes sourced from different systems and we may get different values in different parts of the organization (always a source of trouble). What we could do with our shiny new accounting system is source these reports directly from the accounting system, so we are certain that we get unaltered data. Besides, it is one step less in our landscape: instead of extracting the data from accounting and importing it in the Data Warehouse and then produce the reports there, we directly produce the reports from the accounting system. That is a simpler and thus generally assumed to be a better architecture[*]. Less can go wrong, for instance, it is more robust in an operational sense.

So it is decided and implemented.

A few years later, the system is up and running, something happens that we did not take into account. Either the lawmaker, or the regulator of our industry, or maybe even the clients themselves decide that it is not a good idea that pension funds depend on a single asset manager. Say, the regulator adds a new rule that says that a pension fund may not have more than 70% of its assets at a single asset manager. Suddenly, 30% of our assets move to other asset managers. That is not all that bad, because 30% of the assets that are managed by the competition can move to us. In any case, our 'full service' proposition (fiduciary management) still stands. We still want to handle the pension fund's reporting to the regulators for them, for instance. The pension fund agrees, and orders its other asset manager to do a daily dump of the assets they manage for the pension fund to us so we can do 'client management' next to our own 'asset management'.

But — surprise, surprise — when that stream arrives, it contains swaptions and mortality rate swaps! And we're in trouble, because we are sourcing the pension fund's reports from our accounting system and the accounting system cannot handle swaptions and mortality rate swaps. As a result, we need to move the pension fund's reporting, to the Data Warehouse system after all.

This is for instance the basis of Roger Sessions' interesting anti-complexity approach *Simple Iterative Partitions* which he describes in his book *Simple Architectures for Complex Enterprises* [Ses08]. Sessions literally says that his *definition* of a good architecture is a simple architecture.

Robustness under uncertainty

If we had chosen to do reporting from the Data Warehouse in the first place, we could have more easily adapted to this new situation: just add the stream from the other asset manager to the Data Warehouse and adapt the reports.

Is it fair to expect that we should have chosen the route via the Data Warehouse initially when we implemented the new accounting system? We did not know what was going to happen in the future, did we?

But what if, for instance, it had been known that the option to force pension funds to split their assets was under discussion somewhere. That would not have made it a *certainty*, or a *current* requirement, but it would have made it a known *un*certainty which we could have chosen to take into account. And it probably would have been a known uncertainty, because such policy measures by government regulators do not appear out of thin air one day; they generally are preceded by lots of discussions in various circles, discussions your organization is most likely aware of.

Actively looking for uncertainties[*] and deciding if you take them into account when planning for the future is the core of the powerful strategic planning method called *scenario planning*[†]. Scenario planning is a method to discover and analyze your uncertainties and devise your strategies accordingly. The idea behind scenario planning is that you can

---

[*] Including trying to imagine those that are not already visible in discussions in your industry.

[†] Using scenario planning in a business setting was pioneered by Shell in the 1970's. See Peter Schwartz' book *The Art of the Long View* [Sch97] for a good introduction.

devise strategies that are *robust under uncertainty**. Given that enterprise architecture, as we have seen in chapter 4 has so many 'unknowables' and so much uncertainty, it is a discipline where the strategic method of scenario planning works much better than either forecasting or backcasting.

It is for that reason that the most important part of any future state architecture document must be the inventory of uncertainties that can have a large impact on your landscape. These uncertainties must be agreed upon by the top management of the organization and then handed to the architects to take into account when they design the changes. In other words: you do not give the project architects a desired future landscape (which is not coming to pass anyway), but you give them the uncertainties they have to take into account when designing the next step. It is design guidance at a higher level. In the example of the previous section, if the architects had been given the uncertainty 'potential forced split of assets of pension funds to multiple asset managers' and the command to take that into account, they probably would have designed the setup such that reports would have been created in the Data Warehouse system in the first place, even if that is slightly more complex than creating the reports from the accounting system. In the current reality, that would be an 'unnecessary' extra step, but seen from the scenario perspective, it is a robustness-building choice. Making those kind of strategic choices that have a direct effect on the day-to-day design choices makes enterprise architecture worthwhile.

Or consciously take a gamble.

In many organizations, the 'business' seems to assume[*] that the IT-landscape is as easy to change as its strategy, or even easier. The illusion of the speed of change in the IT world plays a role in this assumption. But if you talk with a company director and ask: "Do you want the designers to nail, screw, and weld you to your current strategy?" they will most vehemently deny that they want this. In which case you can tell them that if he or she does nothing about it, the architects and designers in the projects *will* glue them to the current strategy anyway, with a web of solutions that on average have a life span of fifteen years each. You cannot solve that on the work floor, top management *must* get into this act. Because when you go to the designers and architects in the projects and tell them they should *not* follow the current strategic goals of the organization (e.g. in our example 'security and simplicity'), they will accuse you (and rightly so) of trying to usurp the board's role.

So, using the organization's current strategy combined with backcasting from an imagined ideal future state as the starting point for enterprise architecture (a standard approach) is flawed for a number of reasons. One is that in most cases uncertainties are making the approach basically unsound. Ironically, one of the most pregnant uncertainties is the strategy of the company itself. Systems have an average life time of fifteen years. The strategy of a company manages maybe four. In other words: in the time that the architecture of a system and a large part of its surrounding systems exists, the organization's strategy will have changed four times[†],

---

[*] Insofar as this is part of their discussions at all.
[†] Often following changes in upper management.

and often such changes are pretty radical. If your 'security and simplicity' strategy (no weird products in our portfolio) changes to 'world champion return on assets' (which requires those weird assets) and your accounting system cannot handle it, your new strategy is in trouble*. Do not take your uncertainties into account, and you will most likely end up in a chaotic landscape full of ugly workarounds.

It is therefore a fundamental flaw in many enterprise architecture approaches that one starts from the (current) business strategy and/or a set of principles that may be derived from that strategy. Such a waterfall almost never works.[35]

That does of course not mean that the current strategy plays no role whatsoever. We should certainly not devise solutions that are in conflict with it. But simply taking the current strategy and hand that to the architects to turn it into the starting point of enterprise architecture will almost certainly fail, because the strategy is going to change long before the results of enterprise architecture are visible. What it does mean, is that the board of a company *must* steer enterprise architecture more directly. It must take a longer view so it can direct matters that do not immediately depend on just the *current* strategy and *current* environment. Profiting from enterprise architecture requires a higher level of strategic

---

This is also why it is wise to decide upon (the execution of) a new company strategy only after an assessment what this change means for the landscape — something that currently almost never happens in organizations. This is also because the IT-part of the organization generally has very low status, something that is discussed in other places of this book.

thinking for the organization*, and this also makes it more difficult for enterprise architecture to be successful.

It is ironic, that — while everybody is convinced that IT is changing so rapidly — many IT *landscapes* are so full of inertia that an organization's strategy may change much quicker than IT. IT does change rather quickly, that is true. But that does not mean that the Business-IT *landscapes* are so easy to change. As most enterprise architects know: this requires a way of designing that landscape with the flexibility built in. But their approach to flexibility is often mainly only technical: use enterprise services buses, service oriented architectures, partitioned architectures, software defined infrastructures, et cetera. Apart from the fact that these methods still can result in a mess of loosely coupled dependencies†, and all other sorts of problems such as performance and security issues, they are not specific for the *type* of uncertainty organizations have. Using scenario planning at least gives you an instrument to handle the uncertainties more intelligently and specifically, instead of just going at it with a generic approach that must be able to address everything.

Other aspects

While employing scenario analysis as the basis for future state architecture, and using 'accepted uncertainties' as the preferred way to guide the organization's architects during

---

* And definitely beats the 'blame game' that developers often have employed against users, based on volatile user demand, as described on page 24.

† As illustrated in "Prologue: Loosely Coupled Spaghetti" on page 7.

their design work for specific (i.e., project) goals are most important for an effective architectural approach to the future, there are still the classical choices that can be made and that are important.

Matters like preferred platforms, preferred architectural patterns et cetera can still help. For instance, the architectural pattern 'exception-based architecture' says that — if possible — business processes are automated and that humans are only used to handle the exceptions that the (by definition brittle, limited and inflexible) logic of the systems cannot handle. Such a pattern can be a preferred pattern, and as such written down. But more than a preference, this cannot be. Because sometimes, changing a bit of human processing into automation can have huge consequences that are far more expensive to the organization than employing a few humans is.

Furthermore, for the coming years, based on strategic choices, life cycle management events (e.g., a platform or application going out of support) and so forth, landscape choices can be made at high level. If your data warehouse system is almost end of life, you know you have to do something — and it is a choice for the long term. That too is the moment to look at alternatives, e.g., changing other parts of the landscape to build a better position on the enterprise chess board. Also, from an architectural standpoint, some order of change might be preferable over another order of change. These kind of 'rough' decisions about the landscape are good input for an organization's project portfolio process.

*Architecture is not a profession for the
faint-hearted, the weak-willed, or the short-lived*
Martin Filler

Architecture is always political
Richard Rogers

7 Hurdles

IF THERE WAS to be an 'enterprise chess' manifesto, it would contain:

- Scenario planning over fore- and backcasting
- Requirements over principles
- Collaboration over division of labour
- Design skills over design principles
- Structured documentation (models) at the core
- Risk based abstractions
- A 'checks & balances'-based architecture governance

These together give an organization the means to fight complexity instead of freezing when confronted with it, or fleeing into make-believe simplified worlds. And, before we get into the subject matter for this chapter — the negative territory of things that can go wrong, the positive must be stressed: when it works, it is a lot of fun, because you get the feeling of actually getting something concrete done and you are constantly doing positive things: trying to find the best next step for your organization (instead of just trying to prevent the organization from doing boneheaded things).

However, if complexity is addressed in the way suggested in this book, somewhat analogous to the way chess masters handle the complexity of chess, an enterprise architecture initiative can still fail. For one, the approach in this book has its own preconditions that need to be fulfilled, and (above all: behavioral) areas of extreme difficulty. Some of these hold for any enterprise architecture approach, some are specific for this approach. Some major issues are described below. These might be considered like factors outside of chess, that may influence the game in a negative way. If playing chess requires concentration, and concentration for you means silence, loud music may influence your game in a negative way. If someone keeps part of the chess board hidden from your view, you're playing with a handicap and it will be impossible to find the best moves and check them.

Lack of Board Commitment

Enterprise architecture, as an organizational entity, is at best a small, dedicated, centrally positioned team. As argued before, what it does is represent the 'overall landscape' goals of the organization* in the checks and balances between architectural goals and the goals of change initiatives such as projects. This checks and balances based governance must produce the alignment of individual project goals (and other subdomains of the organization) with the overall landscape goals. Individual project goals are however very difficult to steer from outside the project. A project has a budget, a clear target, commitment of higher management, time pressure, a large team, and so forth. In fact, the large project is often like a supertanker and enterprise architecture is like a small pilot boat. On power alone, this small pilot boat is not going to change the direction of the tanker one inch.

---

* Which, if defined intelligently, contain the key strategic uncertainties to take into account.

In the world of harbors, the harbors have given the pilot the power of command. The pilot comes aboard the tanker and takes over. But that is not what we can do in enterprise architecture, mostly because the demands of architecture — both project and enterprise — are far too complex to let at any stage one rule the other. Running a tanker may be complex, the *requirements* of tanker and harbor are aligned and simple: get the boat quickly and safely in its intended position.

In the world of enterprises, the 'confrontation' of different know hows and different stakeholders must be our instrument to come to the right 'enterprise chess' moves. To get a subdomain of the organization (e.g. a project) to play along with that — from its own perspective: inefficient — process, it needs to be 'forced'. It is only when the enterprise architecture processes have been established for a longer period that such force is not necessary anymore. For enterprise architecture, this means that its role and statements *must* have the backing of the authority that is in the end the owner of its goals: the board, which is owner of the overall landscape goals*. If enterprise architecture says to a project that it

---

This assumes that we have a board that already understands that the complexity of the Business-IT landscape, and above all the complexity and brittleness of IT, is a subject that needs their real attention in the first place. If, for instance, board members have so little insight in the IT field that they are of the (hidden) conviction that technology is 'never the problem', but that, say, it is all an organizational (or behavioral) problem if projects succeed or not, then it will be difficult to get support for attacking the problem of essential complexity of the Business-IT landscape. And sadly, there are still many executives that are unaware of the real problems that come from the complexity of the Business-IT landscape. Such executives tend to blindly believe that IT's possibilities are without limits. And thus they tend

should take the uncertainties that are described in the future state architecture document into account when designing solutions, these uncertainties must come with board approval. If the board has not given enterprise architecture a strong position by demanding that any project plan has a project architecture reviewed by the enterprise architecture function, and if the board does not enforce a government where enterprise architecture 'no go' are resolved[†], projects will spend their energy on staying their own — limited — course, not taking the 'overall landscape' into account.

Without clear commitment of the board, one will end up in an endless discussion on *if* instead of *how* we take the overall landscape requirements into account.

One of the arguments often heard against giving enterprise architecture a position of power (through governance rules, mainly) is that enterprise architecture must not be like the police[‡] or a dictatorship, it must convince on the quality of its arguments. Sometimes, people even go as far to see enterprise architecture as some sort of *support* for projects, helping them out in providing rules and guidelines that are useful for the projects to get ahead[**]. In fact, this approach

---

to believe in new silver bullets — such as the Cloud[*] — and they have to conclude that their IT people are just too inferior to create the solutions.

[†] If need be, up to board level.

[*] Cloud is real enough and will seriously change landscapes and so will the methods that have been tweaked to produce cloud solutions, these days commonly gathered under the moniker DevOps (agile development and operations for IT providers). But that does not mean cloud is without complexity. See also appendix A.

[‡] A comparison that says something about your idea of 'police' in terms of being helpful versus being repressive.

[**] I.e., to quash the opposition.

completely does away with the essential role of enterprise architecture as the protector of the *overall* landscape goals in the 'checks & balances' role.

If people argue that you should not strive for *power*, but that you should build *influence*, they are missing a point. In organizations, it is almost impossible to get influence without some sort of (backup) power. Yes, it is about influence and not about power. Power is not there so you can wield it and get your requirements fulfilled. Power is there to make sure you cannot be ignored, to make sure you are part of the discussion; power is often required to *enable* influence*. That influence still depends a lot on the quality of your arguments, the way you approach others (cooperative and pragmatic, not as a dictator†), but without the power, it is much easier for the organization to try to ignore than to deal with you. You need some sort of power if you want to become part of (influence) the decision making process.

Some twenty years ago, I visited an organization of IT R&D professionals, who told me they were looking for a new manager of IT infrastructure. Now, given the nature of that organization, all the departments were very skilled in IT, led by IT prima donnas, and they were giving the poor infrastructure people a hard time. The organization had just sacked their manager for infrastructure. He had started a few years before and had demanded that he would be given real power. This, given that the powerless managers of before had

---

Influence without power is the (wonderful) *exception*, not the rule.
Except when the enterprise architecture *governance* is the subject. You do wield the power when you demand that projects actually make a project architecture, that they do follow governance guidelines such as the project architecture guidelines, modeling guidelines, and so forth.

been completely ineffective, they gave him. So, he started to enforce all kinds of IT standardization policies and generally made an enemy of all the prima donnas. Naturally, they threw him out. Of course, the organization decided that the next manager should *not* have this power, thus returning to the previous ineffective setup. The point however is, that without the power, there is nothing the infrastructure manager can 'give away'*. There is no way he will be able to make sure 'infrastructure management' is seen as a real stakeholder, which one has to take into account, and of who the requirements are important for the organization. In other words, it will prevent him from making the requirements of infrastructure something the prima donnas should have to take into account too. Instead of *forcing* them, he must make them *co-owner* of the problem. But without power, there is no way he can move the prima donnas to such a position. In my view, the more real power you have, the less you can often sustainably wield it directly. Their previous manager had tried to directly *wield* his power, and had created a war with the prima donnas as a result (and lost). One should not so much wield power, one should use the *possibility* of influence that comes with it.†

---

* In fact, you need the power in part because you can (as part of negotiations and collaborations) visibly *not* wield it.

† Building influence is akin to making it more worthwhile for others to work with you than around/against you. One can see an organization that is to be influenced in terms of fluid mechanics. The organization, like a fluid, seeks the way of least resistance. So, getting influence requires two simultaneous types of activity: you need to make working *with* you as attractive as possible (pull), while making working around/against you as *unattractive* as possible (push).

Another effect of the lack of real board commitment is that the enterprise architecture *organizational entity* is not accepted as a (delegated) stakeholder. Its *role*, instead of its *message*, will then be constantly put up for discussion, which wastes a lot of energy of all concerned parties.

Now, this is probably the most important hurdle enterprise architecture faces. And this hurdle has become bigger over the years, as enterprise architecture generally has gotten a bad name because it has often not produced the effects it was expected to produce. Organizations generally do not trust enterprise architecture very much. The more enterprise architecture has effectively failed, the less likely a board is to give it any position of power. We have already seen that in a way, as the CIO position in boards has risen more than a decennium ago, but more recently has fallen out of grace more and more*.

In situations where the ones that are to be influenced do not *want* to be influenced, you are thus necessarily constantly making a nuisance of yourself, every time you use the second type of behavior to create that influence. And without that second type of behavior, you are severly handicapped. Just 'seducing' those that have no direct advantage to being seduced (as in reality we are talking different goals and different stakeholders) is not going to work.

So, you can build influence without power, but only in part as if you were a nasty insect constantly buzzing them. They will probably try to swat you. . .So, taking up a job as lead enterprise architect without having real power and trying to build that influence is a risky proposition.
It is not necessary that a board has a CIO position, but it should have a CIO *role* and that role should not coincide with one of the other stakeholders such as COO, CFO, et cetera. If there is no separate position, then it must be a role the CEO fulfills, the CEO being the one ultimately accountable for the overall landscape and the only one being in an independent position with respect to the other mandates. Another option is to have this

Enterprise architecture is in a true Catch-22 position. I know of no other way than that a board becomes convinced of the need, finds someone who understands that this power is not to be wielded as a dictator would, and takes a leap of faith.

There is a mitigating circumstance: in the approach sketched in this book, the power of enterprise architecture is — next to letting the board set strategic requirements such as the uncertainties to take into account — mainly directed at forcing *collaboration* of others in the organization. You are not creating an enterprise architecture dictatorship, you are creating the power to prevent the 'overall landscape' goals to be ignored and you are creating the power to prevent incomplete knowledge to create yet another suboptimal situation in your landscape. You create the power to enforce a decent enterprise architecture *governance*.

If the board of an organization does not visibly take ownership of its side of the checks & balances equation that is connected to changes in your landscape*, enterprise architecture is not going to work. If you also have the orthodox 'design office' variant of enterprise architecture (see page 56), which exhibits a lack of ownership on the other side of the 'checks & balances' equation, you are effectively in limbo with your architecture. It is there, because it is seen as a required element of a functioning organization, but it

---

role attached to the board member responsible for strategy, again under the same separation of duties requirements.

* The checks & balances between the overall landscape goals and the goals of a change initiative such as a project. This is an essential element which is by definition in play in enterprise architecture, even if it is not always recognized as such (see also on page 100).

cannot function properly, because there is no ownership of the goals. If this happens, architectural influence on design decisions is generally insubstantial, and what influence is wielded is easily (and constantly) overruled, especially by management.

Isolationism — Siege mentality

This book argues that the complexity of organizations — of the sort where enterprise architecture makes sense in the first place — is way beyond the maximum complexity individuals, or simple rules and guidelines, or abstract/simplified models, can handle. Therefore, the only way enterprise architecture can be effective in addressing the real problems, is by setting up effective *collaboration* between the 'architects' of various stakeholders, be they departments, projects, et cetera. An obvious weak spot of this approach is thus anything that prevents effective collaboration.

Basically, all stakeholders must see enterprise architecture as part of their *own* interests. This is not automatically the case. Officially, everybody will agree, but as Peter Scott-Morgan's in his insightful book *The Unwritten Rules of the Game** illustrated, the official rules of an organization often do not represent how the organization works in reality. Instead, there are often informal rules that are more important. For instance, if department managers are rewarded purely on their 'local' results and not on the 'overall landscape' or on collaboration with central functions, the chance is that they are only interested in what happens their own domain. Taking

[SM94]

the rest of the organization into account is not their problem, worse even, they will not voluntarily spend time on those other domains by working with/on enterprise architecture. They might support enterprise architecture in speech, but not in deed. Corporate culture, therefore can be working against the collaboration that enterprise architecture requires. In fact, if the culture is 'isolationist' and 'political', one of the signs is a strong demand for a principles & guidelines based approach (which can then be used as a 'weapon' in the political fights).

The most damaging of all the ways collaboration can be prevented is the extreme form of isolationism that is the 'siege mentality'. Let's illustrate with an example:

At one time, there was a large important project. The enterprise architects were looking at the dependencies between several important projects — the overall landscape, but now in terms of the overall 'project' landscape — they wanted to set up a discussion between the architects of several domains and projects about these dependencies and what design choices needed to be made there. They were aware that in this large important project, a business analyst had created a good first analysis of one of the important subjects where multiple projects depended. So they wanted this document as input for their discussion.

They were denied. This was a 'project-confidential' document that was not to be shared outside of the project. Taking that document into the architecture board as input for discussion was tantamount to making it public, so the enterprise architects could not have it. Asked for the reason for this lack of transparency, the following reasoning was given: "This document is not yet final and complete. There may be still imperfections and others in the organization will use that to try to kill our approach. We do not want to discuss our approach with the rest of the company until we are completely done and the approach is perfect. Otherwise, our good approach may be killed off for insufficient reason."

Now, this is an extreme example, a 'worst case' if you like, but it is not that uncommon a pattern in a less virulent form. Domains have goals and especially projects will try to protect their progress by shutting out external (potentially derailing) influences. Every project manager knows that 'scope creep' and other outside changes of targets are major problems in getting to the finish line successfully. It is what old-fashioned project managers do: create a precise as possible target, then guard this with their life*. And the less external influence there is, the more the project manager feels in control of his or her deliverables. So, there is a natural and understandable tendency for domains to be nontransparent to a certain extent, as it is a way to minimize outside influence.

Now, it is of course possible that an immature version of a good idea is killed off because of its immaturity, and not because the idea itself in a mature version is wrong. The basic argument is valid. But taking that scenario as a given is a sign of unhealthy distrust[†], and that is in the end what is the source of the siege mentality. Departments or projects working under the siege mentality see the rest of the organization as 'the enemy at the gates'. They have their plan** and they have a drive to see it through. Only

---

Good project managers, of course, manage the *business case*, not the scope.
Or paranoia. See the next section on trust.

156

fully-formed plans get 'out of the gate' and then the rest of the organization is allowed to take 'shots at it'. If the domain loses an argument, you may hear statements like 'loosing a battle, but winning the war'. In fact, you can recognize the siege mentality by the war-like language that is often being used.

A siege mentality requires a few sources to get to the extreme level of the example given above. First, the domain must be exceptionally convinced of its own superiority in design choices. A certain hubris is needed, especially towards the rest of the organization, who 'do not understand it anyway'. This might seem an exaggeration, but this attitude is not that uncommon, though the amount of hubris clearly will vary. Secondly, there must be fear and uncertainty. Those practicing the siege mentality are unconsciously afraid that they will lose the argument, in fact there is an underlying uncertainty about their own strength of argument. If your are really certain about the superiority of your arguments, if you know your plans are so good that they *will* stand up to scrutiny, you will not be afraid to be confronted with that scrutiny, or with other ideas, even if these ideas are possible less mature than your own. Again, there are levels of uncertainly in play, the worst siege mentalities go together with the deepest hidden fears. The worst of the worst siege mentalities occur when the position of the domain coincides with

---

*◄ Possibly for the entire landscape, effectively creating a second future state architecture in your organization.

a natural tendency for paranoia by its inhabitants, especially the domain's management*.

The siege mentality has a few nasty effects for enterprise architecture. First, it is extremely inefficient. Wrong design decisions, based on a lack of insight or knowledge, that could have been found out in an early stage can stay at the core of a 'domain'† architecture for a long time. Repairing it also becomes troublesome. When the result finally surfaces, (often after very long periods, I have seen stuff being kept under wraps for years) not only is it too late to repair fundamental mistakes, the ones proposing it have so much invested that they will fight to the death‡ to keep it alive.

If you are an enterprise architect that encounters a strong siege mentality and it is effectively supported or condoned by higher management, you can kiss any meaningful collaboration that is required for 'enterprise chess' (or any actual working enterprise architecture approach that is based on the assumption of collaboration) goodbye. The situation is even worse: the siege mentality makes it pretty certain that you are forced into a war situation, you will be under constant attack. One that without proper support from the highest management you will lose. If, in such a situation, you encounter

---

This is a cultural aspect higher management must manage explicitly if it wants a cooperative approach to enterprise architecture.

E.g., a project.

A lack of transparency in an organization also makes it possible for projects to start to lie. In a siege mentality this happens easier and sooner, but also without an extreme siege mentality, a lack of transparency enables lying during the last stages before a project goes under. Recall the project mentioned in chapter 1, which even went as far to let a government minister lie to parliament. But I have seen this happen in more cases of troubled projects.

projects that end up in the 'funnel of (self-)deceit' (projects in the final stages of failure, that lie to the outside world, or even to themselves about their status), probably the only thing you can do is wait until the project collapses*.

Out of sight

If you look at the news every night, it becomes clear to you that people can do terrible things to each other. The world is not a place of peaceful collaboration, but our models of running enterprises — including the 'enterprise chess' model for enterprise architecture — largely assume it is. The fact that bad things happen to people makes that we call people who have a habit to trust everybody and everything *naïve*, and that is generally not seen as a compliment.

If you want to do enterprise architecture in the collaborative way, as is the suggestion of this book, and since collaboration is based on mutual trust, you know that you are up against a fundamental biological/psychological driver for people that they have out of protection: distrust. Enterprise chess assumes a bit of a *naïve* approach. In its most virulent and extreme form, the natural distrust leads to the 'siege mentality' of the previous section, but even if that does not happen, 'trust' remains an important aspect of setting up effective collaboration.

---

* Which such projects almost inevitably do. Though some are able to claim 'success' regardless, by simply stating they have finished and dropping the problems into the lap of (IT) operations — not always the strongest player given IT's low status.

Trust, by the way, is not extremely difficult to build. And it is also not a prerequisite. Often you hear "we need to build trust so we can cooperate", but such statements have it the wrong way around. Trust follows from cooperation, and not the other way around. Without cooperation, trust does not form easily, because trust without some proof of trustworthiness amounts to 'naïveté'. What actively cooperating on something does is provide the cooperating parties with a constant stream of people doing what has been agreed or said, so a constant stream of little 'proofs of trustworthiness'.

Which leads to an important hurdle for enterprise architecture. When enterprise architecture is not present when — for enterprise architecture important — cooperations take place, it does not become part of the trust-building that happens*. If enterprise architecture is not available in project boards, in management meetings, such as board meetings, all of this on a regular basis, enterprise architecture is not able to build trust relations with the environment. You can try to mitigate that by having many individual meetings with stakeholders, but they are an imperfect surrogate. If enterprise architecture is not minimally part of the decision making collaborations, it diminishes the levels of trust towards enterprise architecture and as such becomes a hurdle for setting up the collaborative model. Out of sight is out of mind.

Not all groups are automatically trust-building, sometimes a group is at war with itself. But in that case nothing helps anyway, so we can stick to the 'positive' example.

Nature & Nurture

In antiquity, one of our cultural mainstreams started: humanity went on a path that used logical[36] argument as a litmus test for rationality and meaning. This is often associated with the Greek philosophers Plato and Aristotle. Overall, this has been a very successful cultural strategy. It has brought us science and progress; you would not be reading this book if it had not been so successful.

We, as a culture, are so engulfed by this success, that it permeates our belief system in many ways. Some limits of this approach have already been met for a century or so[*], but our everyday culture has hardly experienced a change. We are still a culture of Plato and Newton, not a culture of Wittgenstein[†] and Quantum Mechanics[‡]. And part of that culture is a deeply embedded belief in the power of clear truths and falsehoods and thus a belief in the 'power of rules'. We think 'intuitive behavior' is clearly inferior to 'logical behavior'. We assume good chess players are above all better in logical thought[**], but they are in fact much

---

[*] And in the years between the old Greeks and now were often already noted by some, but those ideas never entered the mainstream.[37]

[†] Who showed us clearly the limitations of the approach of using *logic* to come to *meaning*.

[‡] Which has demolished the predictable rule-like foundations of individual events in the physical world.

[**] An interesting example is Roger Session's chess example in his book *Simple Architectures for Complex Enterprises* [Ses08] where he points out the strength of a certain move because it partitions the board. Apart from the fact that this interpretation of the move is questionable, we already know from De Groot's research (see chapter 4) that this is not the way *good* chess players think.

better in (intuitive) pattern recognition, in *estimation*. Our intelligence is one of 'skill' more than one of 'reasoning'*, but our culture still has it differently.

As Dreyfus showed (already in 1972) so beautifully in *What Computers (Still) Can't Do*[†], this cultural force makes us believe in things, ironically even without proof, and sometimes in the face of total failure of the assumption. The belief in Artificial Intelligence by digital computers by using heuristics (search strategies), and even a Cognitive Science branch that retro-actively tried to rephrase human intelligence as rule-like behavior, were part of that strong cultural undercurrent. The problem is — as for instance the game of chess shows — that the belief is fundamentally mistaken. Even in the purely logical domain of chess, logical means of decision making are so weak that we need an enormous number of them to have any impact (and it only works in very limited domains).

This cultural bias runs deep in IT and it also runs deep in enterprise architecture and its precursor systems architecture. From Edsger Dijkstra's belief, that formal correctness proofs of software items would create a perfectly trustworthy lower level that would be correct and could be used to express higher order logical elements, to, more recently, Roger Session's Simple Iterative Partitions[‡] there is a strong relation with early Wittgenstein and with the Logical Positivists of the

---

"Humans are better at frisbee than at logic" as Andy Clark's wrote in *Being There* [Cla96]

[Dre92]

[Ses08], which contains many assumptions about perfection, like the perfection of the partitions (that are not reflected in the messy reality that a later Wittgenstein showed our human life to be).

162

first half of the twentieth century and their (failed) followers in AI and Cognitive Science.

The bias is also reflected in other areas related to enterprise architecture. Take for instance the way we handle process descriptions. These too, generally, are of a perfect logical nature, especially when we employ structured notations such as the Business Process Model and Notation (BPMN) modeling language. Such structured descriptions necessarily omit the flexibility of human behavior and how it constantly compensates for the fact that the real world is messy, not ideal*. Another such area is strategy, where these days there are more and more attempts to use modeling to improve it. An earlier mentioned example is the addition of a Motivation Extension to the ArchiMate enterprise architecture modeling language in version 2, which deals with modeling the 'why' of the enterprise, with drivers, goals, requirements and some 'how' items such as requirements and constraints, and principles. The — questionable — idea behind this is that the design of the (target) landscape can be linked to a limited set of clear goals that can be logically structured.

When the use of logic and rules visibly fail, we tend to disbelieve that the rules are the problem, and we try even harder to make it work. There is some of that in the core of enterprise architecture today, based as it is on IT. In IT, the belief in the power of logical structure has been extremely strong. After all, the digital computer is the machine which

---

* Colleague Joost Melsen made a funny and insightful observation: the process of walking is more and less constantly falling over and correcting. Processes in the real world are often like that, certainly those that cannot be automated. Our process execution is also a constant correction towards 'bad things not happening'.

has logical rules as its fundamental mode of operations. There is far more to say about this, but for here it suffices that our existing approaches to enterprise architecture are built upon this foundation. We try to work almost completely with logic and structure, with principles and guidelines, and if they do not work to solve the actual problem, we tend to make more of them* or we try to make them stronger/better, thus copying the behavior of that proverbial imperial Englishman, who — when confronted with a foreigner who does not understand English — will retry speaking English more loudly.

This belief in the power of logical structure is amplified by the fact that IT schooling is necessarily confined to small toy-like example problems that *can* be handled with the logical approach. Universities constantly deliver IT graduates who believe in the power of rules, a fact these students have experienced constantly, but at a small scale. *If* they at all learn the limitations, they generally learn it the hard way over a period of many years working in the real world. But some stubbornly refuse to give up the belief in the face of defeat, some become cynical, and some make a life time career out of it — promoting it as a solution to businesses, where it is a message that is 'cultural music' to the business' ears.

The whole cultural drive is strengthened by the biological/psychological 'flight' reaction (see page 85) to overwhelming problems, such as Business-IT complexity of larger organizations.

Sometimes these rules take the form of trying to create 'ontological' definitions, i.e. definitions of what there is. Examples are definitions of 'service', 'application', 'function', et cetera. in frameworks like TOGAF

In the end, much works against us when we need to see the real problem and not flee into make-believe 'simplistic' solutions. It is a lot to ask from people to make the jump from their culturally and biologically driven belief systems, but enterprise architecture is probably a field that requires at least a little bit of that[*].

It is important to recognize that all these simple, model-based approaches often have value. It *is* important to some-times simplify to be able and to look at the big picture. Edsger Dijkstra's approaches have value in IT, and so have Roger Session's approaches in enterprise architecture. What all of these however not do, is solve our problems with Business-IT complexity, not even the approaches that have been specifically designed to do so. And the belief that these approaches do work, is a serious hurdle for those who want to play 'enterprise chess'.

Low ambition levels

Suppose you have had a bad experience with a building contractor on house improvement, you might get the feeling that decent house improvement is not really doable and you might become skeptic about the whole issue. If somebody comes along and tells you that it really is possible to have a smooth process, your experience will tell you the opposite.

The same happens in enterprise architecture. E.g., many organizations have failed attempts at decent current state architecture administrations. They have spent lots of hours building administrations and models and very little to show

---

[*] Another such a field is Artificial Intelligence.

for it. They may have tried a few times over the last two decennia. So, if you come along and tell them that a good and above all current state landscape documentation is possible by deploying a decent enterprise architecture modeling language (such as ArchiMate) and using the right patterns and approach (such as in the book *Mastering ArchiMate*) to keeping such an administration up to date and in sync with other administrations, they will not believe you. And if they do not believe you, they will also not support you. And without their support, such an initiative is doomed.

And they might be right. Because it is not just management or enterprise architecture that needs to be on board. If the engineering groups that keep your infrastructure running, keep to their own unstructured administration (in spreadsheets, graphics, text) because they can control it, because its size is still such that it can be overseen and managed, and because they do not want to learn a new method, you will not get that 'coherent multi-model' administration that you need for a better insight in the start position for every 'enterprise chess move'. See also appendix B.

Can we succeed?

The first few chapters of this book showed how the orthodox approach to enterprise architecture is largely ineffective and why. A large part of that 'why' lies in the enormous complexity and fundamental unpredictability of what we are trying to manage. The previous sections in this chapter describe other aspects that have a strong relation with failed enterprise architecture initiatives and failed projects. The first one is broadly recognized as essential: Top management must own the need for enterprise architecture. I add to that: top management must understand that complexity is mostly essential and not always avoidable, and believe in enterprise architecture's role to help them manage it.

On a cynical note: maybe enterprise architecture is just too difficult for us humans. Maybe we have met the limits of what we can do. Maybe some things are just a type of chess that cannot be played. Jerry Seinfeld once quipped:

> Marriage is like a game of chess except the board is flowing water, the pieces are made of smoke and no move you make will have any effect on the outcome.

Another quote from Sydney Harris* about realism might help us here to keep the faith:

> An idealist believes the short run doesn't count. A cynic believes the long run doesn't matter. A realist believes that what is done or left undone in the short run determines the long run.

I do not believe we should give up. Like a chess player who creates his end result move by move, we must become enterprise architecture realists, using our skills and, above all, our capability of cooperation to create the virtual enterprise architect that *can* handle the complexity and unpredictability. If we can do that, then I am convinced we will succeed.

---

* See page 77

Dear reader,

this book is part of the 'brave new world' of small publishing operations, made possible by the rise of digital technologies. It therefore almost completely depends on *word-of-mouth* marketing[i], it must succeed on its quality and nothing else.

If you like this book and, above all, if it improved your insight in what enterprise architecture is or should be, yes, even if you disagree with it but the disagreement improved your insights, then please suggest this book to others.

[i] In other words: non-existent marketing budgets. . .

*The interesting thing about cloud computing
is that we've redefined cloud computing
to include everything that we already do*
Richard Stallman

A Low-hanging Cloud

OFTEN, WHEN CHANGES in the Business-IT landscape are required, organizations are confronted with a series of results to achieve, all with a different effort required to reach the intended result. It is common practice to look for 'quick wins' that can be achieved first. An often heard phrase for such easy picking is *low-hanging fruit*.

From various professional perspectives, this approach is circumspect. For instance, agile development methods state that it is important to tackle the most *difficult* use cases for a solution first. After all, basing your foundational design decisions on the easiest use case is a recipe for failure. Chances are, that a bridge designed to get cyclists across needs to be completely redone when the more difficult twenty ton lorries have to be serviced. A bridge designed for heavy lorries, on the other hand, will probably carry the cyclists with ease. In enterprise architecture, this is true as well. Design and develop the easy stuff (such as the business process's 'happy flow') first, and you will probably end up in serious trouble when the difficult work flows — such as all the exceptions* — need to be supported as well.

What is 'cloud computing' anyway? What does actually change when you move stuff 'in the cloud'? Interestingly enough, much stays exactly as it was before. Let me explain.

And there are always exceptions to rules that operate in the real world (as opposed to rules that operate in the logical world).

When you look at a business that is supported by IT, you can use the standard 'layering' that most enterprise architects employ. This layering says that you have a business layer — consisting of processes, roles, actors, et cetera — that sits on top of an application layer, where we find the applications that are used by the business, which in turn sits on top of an infrastructure layer: the servers, operating systems, networks, and other foundational IT elements that are needed to actually run those applications. For instance, a sales manager (business) may use a contact relations management (CRM) application (application), running on his desktop (infrastructure) to store information on his clients. In larger setups, the desktop may be a data center, but by and large this is how the Business-IT relation can be modeled.

So, what happens with this setup when this moves to the cloud? The answer is: basically **nothing**. There still is a business layer (our sales manager with his processes) using an application, which in turn depends on the infrastructure.

The *ownership* of those layers changes, though. If the sales manager uses a cloud-based solution, e.g. he uses an application that runs 'in the cloud', there still is that infrastructure and there still is the application, the only difference is that the application does not run on his own infrastructure anymore. The only thing he still needs is a little bit of infrastructure of himself (an internet link, a browser, maybe a plugin such as Java) to *access* that remotely running application. And he would have needed that infrastructure too if the application had run locally on an application server in the company's data center.

If nothing changes, architecturally, why then is cloud computing growing so fast? Something must change, or we would not be discussing this. Well, something does change, and it is not just ownership.

The reason for the growth of cloud computing is that it brings an economy of scale and an economy of flexibility. The economy of scale is for the provider. If you take the example of the CRM application that runs 'in the cloud', and you look at the architecture of the *provider* of that application, he has basically a very simple landscape. After all, his infrastructure does not need to support many different incompatible systems with incompatible architectures*, he just has a single architecture to maintain, only he has lots of it. For the user of the CRM application, this has the advantage that he does not have to support the complex infrastructure required for this application (application servers, database servers, system support programs, monitoring, logging, auditing, virus protection and other security systems, the list is rather long). If you step over legal issues (such as data protection acts that are national, while the cloud is global, or regulators who try to set rules and necessarily expand them to the service providers you use†) the solution is ideal.

The economy of flexibility is for the client of the cloud-provider. If you provide a web site for your customers, it is very busy between 8:00 and 22:00; you may need many load-balanced servers to handle the traffic. And during peak shopping season, your web shop will be hit very often, on a Monday morning in February, traffic will be slow. But as a web shop, you need to provide enough capacity for peak

---

In the worst case scenario, these are of the *canned* kind. See footnote on page 42.
Or it would become very simple to escape from the rules altogether.

traffic. The rest of the year, that infrastructure and the web applications running on that infrastructure are doing nothing. So, what you really would like is to scale your deployment based on actual demand. Busy time? Switch a few extra servers and the applications running on them online. Quiet time? Switch them off, and not so much switch them off, don't pay for hem while they are switched off. Virtualization has made this possible, and this is what cloud deployment offers.

These economies are driving adoption of the cloud. Everybody wants to push their IT deployment in the cloud (public, private of hybrid) because they do not want to pay for IT running idle.

That will work well, until this cloud system is part of a complex landscape of connected applications. If your accounting system is in one cloud and the inventory system is in another, connecting them will be slightly problematic. This is so because the cloud-application provider's economy of scale requires a homogenous internal landscape: not too much diversity in the landscape, or the whole setup becomes again so complex that the cost becomes prohibitive. So, providing connections to all kinds of different specific environments with different requirements is out. The standard solution rules.

A second scenario where cloud works well is where the software deployed is actually capable to automatically make use of scaled up or scaled down deployment. Just moving your existing software to the cloud doesn't really help, it will only be more expensive. Cloud providers must make a living too, and if you push a server to the cloud and it has to be there all the time (no scaling up and down), you will pay much more than running it yourself. Maybe even two to three times as much.

Using cloud-based applications is currently above all attractive for simple landscapes. Are you a consulting company, and your enterprise architecture is more or less restricted to an office suite, a CRM application and a basic accounting system, the cloud is all you need. Dependencies between the three are minimal and each can be easily provided by the cloud providers. This is probably even true for large consulting firms.

But what if you are an organization with a large and *unavoidably** complex IT landscape, with a myriad of dependencies and many mission-critical custom[†] applications? Application silos in the cloud (SaaS[‡] or PaaS**) will have integration issues. Pushing your infrastructure into the cloud won't help you unless your landscape consists of cloud-aware applications. If not, moving stuff to the cloud infrastructure makes your landscape only much more expensive.

One of the underestimated consequences of the cloud is that your architectural dependencies suddenly cross multiple owners. This means that making coherent, landscape-wide,

---

[*] Because of the business demands.

[†] Either as application or as 'configuration' in a generic platform.

[‡] Software as a Service. A service that provides an end-user program to the customer, without the need for that customer to manage his or her own infrastructure (except basic access to the internet, e.g., via a browser). Examples are Microsoft Office365 or Apple's iWork for iCloud.

[**] Platform as a Service. A service that provides a programmable/configurable application (the 'platform') to the customer, without the need for that customer to manage his or her own infrastructure (except basic access to the internet, e.g., via a browser). An example is Salesforce CRM.

174

architectural decisions — in other words: enterprise architecture — has become more difficult. Was it already the case with using different systems from different providers that you had to live with various *canned* architectures, now suddenly you get a situation that even something as simple as life cycle management is not your domain anymore. An example may make that clear: if cloud-application X is updated to a new version that requires version Y of Java on your desktop, and cloud-application Z cannot work with that version of Java but the provider of cloud-application Z has no plans yet to update, you are stuck. And given the nature of cloud-applications, you cannot postpone updating application X. And this is no fantasy. Already providers like Microsoft and Apple force updates of infrastructure plugins like Flash and Java, for security reasons. What happens if that cloud-application is incompatible with that new version?

The above is a simplified example and cloud providers are already reacting, for instance by providing multiple versions of their offerings in a cloud*. But except in the most simple of enterprise architectures, systems are more than just support for a human that performs a human process. Cloud-based systems for risk management for asset managers, for instance, are already the norm. That is more than just using a browser to access a user interface. Such systems need to be fed with real data from the actual investments and the data and reports they produce must often be fed back into the organization's own systems, such as data warehouses. There, 'cloud' does

---

* Which of course eats into their economies of scale, but let's not get into that.

not only mean 'lower infrastructure cost', but it also means 'more complex connections and dependencies' and so forth.

So, while cloud is going to make it easier and cheaper for the most simple of enterprise architectures, it's going to produce new requirements and extra complexity in large enterprise landscapes, extra complexity that is also more difficult to manage because of the demand-supply boundary that is part of cloud. Cloud, too, will not be a *silver bullet*. Cloud will undoubtedly become an important aspect of the landscape, but the fracturing it promises will probably also produce many headaches in the years to come.[38]

Back to the low-hanging fruit: there are already several cloud-based services, from infrastructure to applications. These figure prominently in brave new worlds, in which businesses expect the cloud is going to enable them to outsource much of their IT operations, or at least make it much simpler. But that seems to be based either on the cloud's obvious advantage for simple enterprise architectures, projected on much more complex landscapes, or on ignoring the fact that cloud *deployment* (IaaS[*]) requires cloud-aware applications to bring any advantage. The cloud is seen as low-hanging fruit, the available services must be profited from, without paying enough attention to the more complex issues.

If you have only limited visibility, in this case because only short distance effects are taken into account, you may safely equate 'quickly picking the low-hanging fruit in the cloud' with 'driving with a high speed into architectural fog'.

Infrastructure as a Service. A service that provides a raw computing environment to the customer, without the need for that customer to manage his or her own data center. Examples are Azure or Amazon Web Services.

Two important characteristics of maps should be noticed. A map is not the territory it represents, but, if correct, it has a similar structure to the territory, which accounts for its usefulness.
Alfred Korzybski

B   Current State Architecture

I **N CHESS, YOU HAVE** full information on the current position when you are 'designing' your next moves. In 'enterprise chess', as we noticed in chapter 4, it is *impossible* to know your current position in full.

It is surprising how little effort most organizations put into knowing their position well. It is not uncommon for organizations to have all kind of independent documenta-tions/administrations of their Business-IT landscape. Most have a Configuration Management Database (CMDB), but many of these are of dubious quality. Most often, all kinds of IT groups have their own administration, mostly in spread-sheets and drawings. Business continuity managers have documentations of the key systems and the processes that rely on them, but you should not be surprised if the processes mentioned in their business impact analyses are different processes from those that are part of the official process documentation in business process manuals. Both business process manuals and business impact analyses may use quite different sets of applications, with different names, different subdivisions and so forth. In short, even if everything in the organization is documented (and this is not always the case), it is just not documented in a *coherent* way.

Many organizations have tried to build a reliable doc-umentation for at least a few purposes (mainly enterprise architecture itself) and have found that this is exceedingly difficult. The main reason is that all these groups on the ground have quite different demands for their documentation. Getting the knowledge synchronized between a central administration and the operations on the ground is also difficult, because the people on the ground do not immediately profit from the effort and because their demands on what is to be documented differ from the central department.

Take for instance a database operations group in your IT department. They know everything to keep the databases up and running, and therefore they need to have knowledge about the underlying infrastructure such as servers and storage. What exactly makes *use* of the database is not a primary concern for them, they work bottom-up, supplying reliable database operation to whatever application is using the database. For their use, a spreadsheet with databases and some information on which servers it runs is enough documentation of their landscape. When there are problems, they can look quickly enough on the servers itself to see how it is configured and so forth, and this direct knowledge is far more reliable than any second hand documentation. If there is a change in their landscape, updating a spreadsheet is quick and easy and fulfills their need.

But for the central administration, it might be useful to know the things that the database group can see directly, things like operating system versions, added support software on the servers and so forth, e.g., in support of lifecycle management. It might be logical to synchronize with the server operations group for that, but these people have their own spreadsheet. And then you run in subtle problems of slightly different names for the same elements, or even that both administrations do not agree. The database group has at one time requested new servers and have then moved some databases on them. The server group, interested in keeping their service up and running, also working bottom-up, may have outdated information about which databases run on the servers as they do not work with these databases daily. And they even are able to switch a database from one server to another without the database operations group noticing.

The seemingly obvious thing to do is to make a superset in a central administration and have this used by people on the ground. But the superset may not be as easily usable because what is useful sub-structure for one only adds unnecessary and irritating detail for another. We are firmly back in Ludwig Wittgenstein territory: *meaning lies hidden in correct use*, and if for a certain group of users there is a lot of unnecessary detail and substructure in information, the meaning for them is damaged. That works in two directions: the CMDB needs *all* the desktops, keyboards, screens and so forth, but from an enterprise architecture perspective the individual screens and keyboards are irrelevant and the desktops can be documented as a small collection of *configurations* (types of desktop). If the central current state architecture has all these CMDB items, it becomes unusable.

The situation is even more complex, as it is also impossible to create that superset and have it used directly by all who need it. Take the help desk system. This system needs information about applications, key users, application managers, possibly about infrastructure required to use the application and so forth. This is all information one can model in an enterprise architecture model. But the enterprise architecture modeling tool will not be the tool that can support the help desk in its daily work. Because the modeling tool of the enterprise architects is not a system that can handle help desk 'tickets' and the work flow that comes with them, for example.

So, the — by definition different — demands from different users lead to the inescapable conclusion that you can never have a single encompassing model somewhere. You will always have *multiple models of enterprise reality*, all providing meaning for different parts of the organization, based on how they are used. And all those different uses requiring different 'models'. It is important to recognize that all these documentations are models. The CMDB is a model, what is in the help desk system is a model, yes even those spreadsheets that the run managers use are actually (weak) models of reality. They may be documented in an unstructured way (text, graphics), slightly structured (spreadsheets) or strongly structured, that only impacts how reliable the structure is, they all are *models*.

So, if you want to have better insight in your start position before making a move, you need to work on getting a coherent set of descriptions and administrations of your landscape. And though a single supermodel is out of the question, such a coherent set can work with a central CSA (Current State Architecture) model that is a central hub in that coherent set.

Such a model only works when it has enough detail. An abstract model of a few business functions and main applications will not cut it. You need a model with *all* applications, *all* servers & infrastructure*, and *all* business

---

* Though one can safely leave all the individual personal computers, keyboards, screens and such out and keep only 'configurations' in the model

processes and what IT they use. Such a model, if designed well, can become very large but still be maintainable. At one time, the enterprise architecture unit I was responsible for had a model of 41,000 elements and relations that was easily maintained by a *single* FTE*.The point is, namely, that the amount of changes in your landscape turns out to be rather limited in the end. Everybody is afraid of the speed with which such an administration (model) becomes outdated, but in reality, your organization is not bringing a lot of changes to production every weekend. Maybe a few servers change and some software upgrades or small installs happen. And once in a while, when a large project goes live, the changes are more extensive, but those are one-off events. In reality, an IT landscape has a lot of inertia[†]. Of course, this is also a matter of smart design of the current state model. Here a design rule may be effective: we only model what we

---

for these. In fact, large but homogenous landscape parts may be safely modeled by *configurations* instead of *instances*. See [Wie14] and the blog http://masteringarchimate.com for several posts about such choices.

There is a single 'conditio sine qua non' for this to work: documenting the landscape *must* be done with structured information (a model) and not with unstructured information (text and graphics). The model referred to was done using the ArchiMate enterprise architecture modeling language. The way this was set up in my practice has led to the book *Mastering ArchiMate – Edition II* [Wie14], which contains both a beginner's introduction to the language, as well as a lot of practical patterns and solutions for typical modeling areas.

We often complain on how hard it is to change the IT landscape and how slow that is. These complaints are far more real than the suggestion believed by most that the speed with which IT changes is high. The experience learns that the amount of work required to model the changes is very limited. The only problem is setting up the situation that these changes reach the modeler in a reliable way.

can keep up to date with a maximum of one FTE. So, if the current process descriptions are word processor documents with graphics, do not add them to your current state model. There is no way you can keep up with any changes, even if the documents are coherent enough to put in a model. In a case like that, the people documenting the business must change to a more structured documentation (e.g., BPMN models) that can be aligned with the enterprise architecture model.

From documentation to production

If you really have a very good structured documentation of your landscape, there comes a point you can even use that documentation in your operations. One interesting example is the use of this information for identity and access management. Suppose you have your enterprise architecture landscape (the CSA) modeled in enough detail in an Archi-Mate model. And you have your business processes modeled in BPMN (in a Current Process Structure, or CPS), but you add to that BPMN that you can link items from your CSA to items in your CPS*. Your CPS contains process models that contain the relation between roles and activities. And you add to that relations between activities and applications services (from the CSA) used. As a result, you can derive which roles use what applications services. And finally, you have an administration (in IAM tooling) that couples identities (persons) to roles. This gives you the basic information to provide

---

* Such a mapping is described in [Wie14].

authorization for application services derived directly from your structured business processes documentation.

Such a coupling between these domains becomes possible if the domains are modeled instead of just written down in an unstructured way (word processor documents et cetera). It is attainable if you use structured documentation (models) for your administration of your business process and IT landscape and it is also doable. But it requires a very well designed structure of all these administrations.

In most cases, you will still have several systems that are technically independent, but where you can make sure the world they describe are one logical world. You set up these administrations in master-slave or synchronized setups. E.g., if your CMDB is leading for information about your technical infrastructure (servers and such), you make it the source of truth for your CSA via a technical coupling (e.g., export from one and import into the other).

All of this is work and it takes time and money. But if done right, you also save a lot of effort and you minimize risk. Projects start with a far better knowledge of what they are going to change, so there are less surprises along the way. Preparations of larger life cycle management changes in your infrastructure become easier, as you already know which elements in your landscape depend on the ones that are to be updated. All the work that is done over and over again, is done with less effort and with higher quality.

In life, as in chess, forethought wins
Charles Buxton

Chance favours the prepared mind
Louis Pasteur

C Future State Architecture

A FUTURE STATE Architecture can be updated once a year. It is important to revisit the material in it once a year, including executive board discussion to make sure the organization remains focused on the 'long view' that is required for enterprise architecture.

1 Executive Summary — Which landscape suits us best?

2 Hard Boundaries

Certain choices for the long term may be hard. Here you list the strategic requirements for all projects to take into account. Possible entries are mainly standards to adhere to. E.g., the use of certain compliancy standards, security and risk standards, et cetera. These are choices that under *no* circumstance will be put up for discussion and exceptions must be confirmed by the board of the organization.

3 Current strategy and its consequences

The organization has a current strategy. The consequences of the current strategy for acceptable or even required developments in the Business-IT landscape are described here. Example: if the company moves from a B2B to a B2C strategy, a consequence could be that a consumer-oriented web presence must be developed.

4   Potential Developments — Uncertainties

This section contains a list of identified uncertainties under which the future design decisions must be robust. This list is used by the project architect and enterprise architecture to check his design against. The list must be confirmed by the executive board of the company, who are also major contributors in a 'scenario planning' exercise. You do not need a full scenario planning exercise, though if your organization already does this, it is a great start.

Every uncertainty is described with a number, a name, a description of consequences for the Business-IT landscape if it goes either way, level of impact (high/medium/low) and level of uncertainty (high/medium/low). The most important uncertainties have high impact and medium to high uncertainty or high uncertainty and medium to high impact. The low uncertainty ones can be listed as a 'prediction', the low impact ones can be ignored.

5   Potential Future Landscapes

Here, the strategic choices and uncertainties are used to develop a number of potential solutions of which one is chosen as the preferred one. The others are context for the project architects that use this document in their projects. If possible they take these into account.

6   Road Map Suggestions

Based on what we already know what needs to be done. E.g., from uncertainties we want to be robust under, from strategic choices that have been made, we suggest from an architectural perspective what order of large changes in our landscape is best.

Design is a plan for arranging elements in such a way as best to accomplish a particular purpose
Charles Eames

All that matters on the chessboard is good moves.
Bobby Fischer

D Project (Start) Architecture

HERE IS an example of what could be a Project (Start) Architecture (or PSA) Guidelines document*. This example is (slightly) based on an organization using the PRINCE2 project management method, as it refers to PRINCE2 products (such as *Project Brief* ('charcoal' business case and plan) and *PID* (project plan). It can easily be adapted to link with other project management methods.

1 The goal of a Project Start Architecture

Projects facilitate the implementation of change in the organization. They do so by delivering business solutions. The architecture of a project is the design of the business solution that it is going to deliver, given its scope and business requirements. The Project's Start Architecture is the description and model of that design, as documented at project start. Its goal is to provide tangible and SMART support for steering and governing the change implementation. Thus, the PSA is an instrument that supports governing and steering changes which are implemented following a project approach.

Depending on the type of project that is being prepared, the creation of a PSA can be organized differently. For large programs, it could even be a project of its own. In any change initiative there will be one or more milestones where (a specific part of) the architecture is elaborated to be ready for an implementation. The

Adapted from an existing PSA guidelines document, reused with permission.

guidelines in this document have been defined with that reference in mind

Although this document suggests a table of contents of subjects to include in a PSA document, a project may choose to organize architecture content differently. For easy reading of this document, we assume all architectural content is in a single PSA document which follows the proposed structure. However, the guidelines refer to the project's architecture irrespective of its form: if the project chooses to describe it in multiple documents, the guidelines apply to that set.

There is almost always a phase preceding the project where scope and business requirements are not yet fixed (at least partly). For larger projects this could be in an initial business case or project brief phase, for smaller initiatives there would be an analysis phase. It is advisable to already document the knowns and unknowns in such a phase in a 'charcoal sketch' PSA. There are multiple reasons why that is advantageous:

- It allows for interaction on conditions, achievability, uncertainties and architectural risks which may be included in decisions regarding business requirements and scope;
- It allows for early (informal) verification of the architecture with stakeholders;
- Such an effort usually helps in stabilizing the context in which the project is going to be executed;
- It reduces the effort to create a PSA before project start.

It is quite common that also at project start, there are still uncertainties, unknowns, and architectural risks. These may stem from the environment, dependencies on other work for the project, and/or missing information at the time of writing. The essence is to pragmatically but consciously manage them, which may e.g. imply providing incremental updates to the project architecture during the project.

In short, the PSA:

- Acts as a basis/input for composing the plan for a project (it is input for the "Initiating Project" phase in the PRINCE2 method).
- Contains the basic design* of business (products, organization, processes)†, software, data,and infrastructure; it is the guiding framework for further elaboration of the solution to be delivered in a project, and should e.g. be useable for coordination of further analysis and design within the project.
- Is maintained during a project (following versions are named Project Architecture (PA) instead of Project Start Architecture), so that at project end it is the exact reflection of what needs to be operated and managed by the support organization.
- Defines intended changes by identifying them with respect to the existing architecture, which is reflected in the 'current state architecture' model; see [1]).
- Contributes to the future architecture. The PSA can be seen as the specification of an area that the future state architecture landscape as a whole has identified on a conceptual level (see [2] for the most recent future state architecture description).

The PSA is used in three ways:

- It documents the solution to be delivered by the project (it can be a framework for project execution). If a project is broken down into phases (stages, increments), the PSA may

---

* It is impossible to precisely prescribe a required level of detail here, because that strongly depends on the project. Whenever directions given are less detailed, this leaves room for uncertainty and interpretation. The project architecture should provide the project with enough and sufficient description and modeling, such that the remaining uncertainty and freedom falls within acceptable project risks. Please refer to the checklist in Chapter 3 of these guidelines.

† Generally, this is not a subject of detailed review. The business is in charge of which processes we must have. But knowing which processes are to be supported is input for the rest of the design, and looking at completeness is one main issue that can be reviewed.

include solution definitions per phase. It should however contain a clear basic design for the target state, i.e. the state to be achieved after the last project phase. In practice, the further ahead the target state, the harder it tends to be to specify the architecture (the architect's daily headache). In the PSA, this can be mitigated by (self-)assessing the robustness and quality of the target state architectural design versus the upfront known additional requirements, and different kinds of uncertainties (e.g. functional, technical, dependencies).

- It may identify changes that are required in the enterprise architecture of the organization. For example: the project may have a sound reason to deviate from a direction identified in the Future State Architecture or in agreed guidelines/standards.
- It supports how to be ready for handover of project results to the support organization (Ref. [3]).

There might be exceptions were a project is about such a large and complex change to the landscape that this standard ordered setup cannot easily be applied. If that is the case, a project and Enterprise Architecture can make specific agreements about how the PSA will come to be.

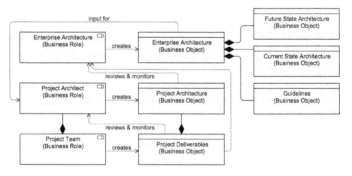

Figure D.1 Relation between EA and Project

The diagram on page 192 illustrates the architectural context of a project architecture. The project architect creates the project architecture which is reviewed by enterprise architecture (after discussion in the architecture board). If during the project, the solution architecture changes, this must be reflected by the project architecture. Therefore, the project architect must monitor and review the actual design decisions being made in the project (or make them). The EA function monitors any changes in the project architecture and at the end of the project will review the project results to see if they conform to what was in the project architecture.

2   What is a Project (Start) Architecture?

2.1   What is a PSA used for?

From the previous chapter, one can deduce that the PSA contains the project result's design, such that it allows

- A PID to based on it (creating a PSA should precede creation of a PID*)
- A project architect to guide and monitor project execution
- Guidance to the project team members and stakeholders to guide further analysis and design
- The lead architect to monitor that the project's result fits in our enterprise architecture.

In a preparation phase, a 'charcoal sketch' PSA can contain the concepts, basic design choices etc. to support business case and project mandate (including e.g. proposed scope/requirements decisions to make in that respect).

In addition to the above, a PSA can be used for other communication purposes.

One should realize that this can be a substantial activity which may also require planning.

2.2   What is the scope of a P(S)A?

What to include in a PSA is determined by crossing out: after a project result has gone into production, the organization must have a complete and functioning landscape. So the project architect considers the current & target landscape minus the parts that are not affected by the project. If starting with this broad perspective, there is less risk of uncoordinated dependencies (or 'white spots').

The time horizon of a PSA is the intended end state for the landscape. Every phase that goes live separately is described in the PSA (this is a 'plateau'), because it is part of the complete and functioning landscape of the organization at that point in time*.

In terms of subjects: a PSA covers all details required for a phase in the project†. Everything that is left out must be left out based on an assessment that leaving it out:
- Does not result in unacceptable risks for project success
- Does not result in unacceptable risks for the landscape as a whole

2.3   Which subjects belong in a PSA?

The subjects described in a PSA are derived from its goals: creating an architecture for the project that by architectural design identifies the target solution while taking into account the uncertainties,

---

* The organization must remain operational while the landscape is changed. Change in IT is often of the 'rebuilding the ship while at sea' kind.

† Note: this includes architecture for exploitation (e.g. backups) after 'go live'. See [3] for Support Guidelines. There is no way to give a fixed proper detail level for a project, but the risk assessment mentioned gives a proper guidance for deciding which details are important or not.

unknowns, and architectural risks that the project has to deal with.[*]
In addition, the PSA can help to manage the consistency of the
enterprise-wide architecture.

So, the PSA should address the following subject, being transparent on subjects for which information is not yet sufficiently available
in the first version:

- Subject matter introduction:
  Any background information that is relevant knowledge for
  understanding the project and the more structured parts of
  its architecture. This is informational only and not a matter
  for review and it is intended to improve understanding of the
  actual design choices made.

- Solution Architecture:
  The description of elements that form the structure (how does
  it work) and behavior (what does it do) of the solution — not
  necessarily identifying all internal details, but with enough
  explanation to demarcate the interaction of the solution elements in our landscape and to manage the risk related to the
  architecture of these elements:

  − The business and information architecture contains rele-
    vant actors and roles, business functions, business processes,
    business objects. It should be clear how any of these ob-
    jects are changed or affected.
  − The same holds for the application and data architec-
    ture. Objects contained: application services, application
    functions, application components and data objects.

The uncertainties, unknowns, and architectural risks may stem from the
environment, dependencies on other work for the project, and/or missing
information at the time of writing. The essence is to pragmatically but consciously manage them. As already stated in the previous chapter, this may
imply incremental updates to the project architecture.

      – Likewise for the infrastructure architecture. Objects contained: infrastructure services, devices, nodes and technical artifacts*.

For modeling the above in ArchiMate, please refer to modeling guidelines as in [4] and [5].

It would in principle be possible, that a project affects but does not change an architectural layer. (Re)modeling that layer is in that case superfluous.[†]

- Specification of the solution:

A solution can be significantly influenced by business requirements aimed at its quality of operation (monitoring and assuring correctness of its operation). We call these requirements 'control objectives.' This is typically a category of requirements that is defined in later project stages (although that does not always do justice to the impact that such requirements may have, so there's an uncertainty that the project architect may have to deal with). These control objectives and their corresponding measures are specified with the relevant objects in each architecture layer. The following control objectives need to be modeled in a PSA:

      – *Business Continuity*: business processes have the following 'control objectives:'

           ★ MTPD (Maximum Tolerable Period of Disruption);

           ★ RTO (Recovery Time Objective);

           ★ RPO (Recovery Point Objective)

From these, requirements can be derived which apply to IT. However, business continuity 'control objectives'

---

* Please note, that the infrastructure architecture is usually defined in co-operation with ICT. Also note, that implementation specifications usually become available during project execution.

[†] As an example: replacing a data delivery or replacing a standard software solution does not necessarily impact business processes. However, the architect should take care to also consider maintenance processes, such as data management and systems management processes.

implementation could also be limited to the business level.

- *Information Security*: the familiar classifications confidentiality, integrity, and availability.*
- *IT Service Management*: service levels specifications should be based on the control objectives availability capacity, security, and IT continuity. The 'units of service' to which they apply can very naturally and consistently relate to one or more objects in the architecture model when that is being constructed (Ref. [5]).
- *Regulatory*: all architectural layers can be impacted by regulatory control objectives.

These control objectives are specified by various stakeholders in various documents. They need to be modeled in the PSA because of handover to the support organization (since the current state architecture model is leading for service management, this includes handover of the project model to current state architecture maintenance). On a more detailed level, other quality requirements† may also apply to application services and infrastructure services. Think of e.g. data volumes, response times, and processing throughput. If there are critical requirements amongst these, they deserve attention in the PSA. The PSA needs to clearly define, how 'controls' realize the above mentioned 'control objectives.'

- Requirements related to project dependencies:
  If there are design choices to make and/or solution elements to be created outside the scope of the project, but with relevance for the project at stake, these are identified. This

---

Most current classification guidelines can be obtained via the Information Security Officer. See also . . .for general security policies.

These are commonly referred to as 'non functional' requirements. We find that misleading terminology, because they always relate to conditions relevant to the business, and prefer to name them quality requirements.

allows those items to be managed as dependencies in the PID. Note: how to manage/operate a solution should always be part of a project's scope, rather than a dependency.

- Design choices:
  These are documented per architecture layer and — if relevant — per object. May consist of principles, guidelines, standards, an assessment of alternatives, should always contain the rationale and clarification how to implement the design. There are many subjects and areas to consider, it is up to the project architect to decide relevance. As a reminder, don't forget about fellow change disciplines such as versioning and testing, and operations:
  - *Units of deployment*: choice can be influenced by requirements on integration, scalability of deployment, or even on module independence with regard to testing;
  - *DTAP environments*: make sure to design DTA environments and fulfill preconditions to allow all required types of testing.*

  Please note: Security is an integral part of the architecture: security related objects are therefore included in the design; security classifications and security requirements are an integral part of the solution specification. There is no separate 'security architecture'.

2.4 Which elements to create a PSA from?

The following three products comprise the primary input for a PSA.

---

* It so happens, that production environments such as fail-over or backup are used for acceptance testing because testing preconditions cannot be met in other environments. This conflicts with regulatory requirements (and with common sense) and is not allowed — unless explicitly allowed by Security Officer, Business Continuity Manager, Lead Architect and Support Organization.

1. *The Enterprise Architecture*, consisting of:
   * Future State Architecture (FSA) [2] (link available at the end of this document) — provides direction for a few years to come; is specified at a relatively high level of aggregation and contains requirements for solution designs (e.g. which business goals and uncertainties to take into account when designing);
   * Current State Architecture (CSA) [1] (link available at the end of this document) — contains the structured documentation (models) of the current situation, provides the baseline for a project, contains a lot of detail;
   * The 'body of choices' of previous analyses and discussions which form the standards and guidelines we work with (link available at the end of this document).
2. *(Approved) Project Brief*
   This contains the business case for the project and a rough plan how to execute the project, including an estimate of staffing, governance and financial resources required for execution. The project brief will also normally contain a rough sketch of the desired solution - possibly already in the form of a 'charcoal PSA' - since that is required to be able to arrive at the initial full business case that PRINCE2 prescribes.
3. *Subject matter expertise*
   Change and modernization inherently require expertise to arrive at good insights, which are prerequisite inputs for robust design. The existing, documented architecture (future state and current state) is 'only' the starting point. Next to architecture, there may be other valuable sources of information, such as
   * Process manuals or models;
   * Earlier analysis and design documents;
   * Software manuals and other vendor information;

★ Service management documents;
★ Et cetera.

2.5 How to create models?

Architecture models are created on the basis of the ArchiMate* structure, which leads to a division into the following layers:
- Business and information-architecture (what does the organization do, and with what (abstract) information)
- Application- and data-architecture (how are the business processes supported by applications and how is business information represented as data in applications)
- Infrastructure architecture (how are the applications supported by infrastructure and how is application data represented as low level artifacts such as databases)

For every layer, it contains an elaboration of
- Active structure: who/what are the processing elements;
- Behavior: what processing is there;
- Passive structure: which elements are subject to processing.
- This ArchiMate-structure is guiding for ordering the contents of a P(S)A.
- In order to model consistently across the organization, models adhere to the Modeling Guidelines Project Architectures [4] and to the Modeling Guidelines Current State Architecture [5] where modeling directions (including for instance which details can be omitted from models and which patterns to be used) are given.

When modeling, the project architect can make use of Current State Architecture objects in his/her baseline.

---

* ArchiMate is a simple yet effective language, in which all relevant architecture elements with their mutual relations can be modeled. The ArchiMate language is a leading worldwide standard, governed by The Open Group. See http://www.opengroup.org/archimate/ for additional information.

2.6 Which standards to use?

To allow easy coordination and communication of the PSA and derived deliverables with other stakeholders, the project architect should reuse definitions from existing master information sources:

- BIA classification (owned by the business continuity manager (Ref. [6]);
- CIA classification (owned by the information security officer (Ref. [7], [8]);
- ORM policies* (owned by the operational risk manager (Ref. [9]; practical translation to a risk matrix is available, see Ref. [10]);
- Common Process Structure† (owned by the lead business process manager);
- Current State Architecture (owned by the Lead Enterprise Architect (Ref. [1]; please contact an EA team member to achieve relevant information).

Please note, that service and support processes will increasingly make use of formalized definitions from these sources. Changes to these sources must be reconciled via their owners. Especially for the Common Process Structure and the Current State Architecture the latter is important to stay aligned: both are constantly updated information repositories, reflecting the dynamics of our environment.

2.7 Who to involve in a PSA?

Writing a PSA is done be the project participant who has the role of Project Architect. He may cooperate with colleagues, for instance:

Please note that the ORM policies prescribe categorization of risk to adhere to the standard categorization. Additionally, policies require that control measure are elaborated. Those that significantly impact the architecture need to be included in the PSA.

The detailed models of our business processes

- Business analysts for the business and information architecture;
- IT specialists (suppliers, DBAs, ICT employees for infrastructure and desktop applications, software specialists) for the application and data architecture;
- Business representatives and project managers when it comes to providing input with respect to scope, focus, priorities, risks;
- Other architects for any of the above, best practices, existing architectures, and any kind of support.

The project architect is responsible for the project architecture and acts in assignment of the project, under the supervision of the project manager. The project executive is accountable for the project architecture.

The Project Board is the primary and only decision platform regarding execution of the PID. It is accountable for dealing with risks and dependencies. Interaction with the project board is managed by the project manager, the project architect may need to advice, either based on the PSA or (in case of e.g. a project exception) an update to it.

The project architect may seek advice with Enterprise Architecture on topics, architectural design issues, or review issues (see remainder of this paragraph). This may contribute to the alignment of the PSA with other architectures and with other initiatives.

Enterprise Architecture and if need be the Architecture Board can be used for informal reviews of PSA-versions, and also for specific design choices of a fundamental nature.

When the project architect has the opinion that the PSA is good enough, he/she asks the Architecture Board to review the project architecture.* The Lead Enterprise Architect creates a formal review based on the review discussion in the Architecture Board. Thus there

---

* The project's planning plays an important role here, according to review milestones as defined in PRINCE2.

is a segregation of duties between execution (project participation) and monitoring (reviewing). Ideally, there is an open dialogue with the project architect when a formal review is composed. This is to be able to mold review comments into advices that are clear and sound enough so that the project can translate them into concrete actions and/or decisions.

The Lead Enterprise Architect formally reviews the PSA and advises the project regarding the PSA. In case the review contains 'no go', the review is considered to be negative and the project is working on the basis of a non-approved PSA. It is the project architect's role to assure transparent insight in the PSA's review status to all project stakeholders (mainly to project manager and to the project board), and also to coordinate follow up on review items. Follow up on review items is per agreement between project architect and Enterprise Architecture.

2.8 How to apply the PSA (life cycle)?

From the moment that the PID has been approved, the Project Start Architecture (PSA) becomes the Project Architecture (PA). As of that moment:

- The business and information architecture from the PA is the leading framework for elaborating business processes and information usage;
- The application and data architecture from the PA is the leading framework for elaborating the application architecture (software architecture) and the data architecture;
- The infrastructure architecture from the PA is the leading framework for TI-level changes.
- The Project is not allowed to realize architecture that is not mentioned in the PA. The PA is then changed and again subject to review.

If the PA needs to be changed during the project, this is done by the Project Architect. In case of changes with substantial impact, it is wise to seek intermediate advice and/or alignment. This does not need to put the project on hold. However, the Project Architect needs to account for eventual acceptance of the PA parts that need to be included in the Current State Architecture at project completion, and by the intended support manager for handover of the project results. The PSA checklist in the next chapter may assist the project architect in assessing impact to be 'substantial' or not.

Again, regular intermediate interaction with Enterprise Architecture is advisable and may contribute to the speedy alignment of the PA.

Together with other relevant solution documentation, the PA is part of handover at final project delivery. The PA models will be included in the Current State Architecture (and decommissioned elements removed). If the solution will require further maintenance, its architecture will be available as baseline.

If it would so happen that maintenance would require a new project to be defined, then that project will have its own PSA. The actual current state will then be a source for that PSA.

The diagram on page 205 contains a BPMN model of the basic PSA creation and maintenance process. Not shown in the figure is the exception that occurs when the project decides to go ahead with an unapproved PSA.

3 A PSA checklist

As already stated throughout this document, it is hard (or even impossible) to exactly specify upfront when a PSA can be considered good enough. One can argue that it is good enough when it proves useful for the purposes of stakeholders it was written for, but that can only be proven afterwards and will not help while writing it.

Second, projects can be of different natures, and managing these projects may require different focus and subjects in the PSA in order for it to be a useful instrument: a large-size project that lasts three years will have to pay more attention to changes in its

205

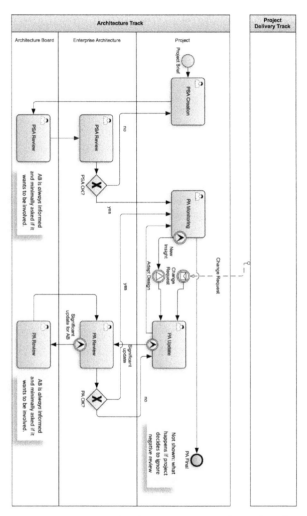

Figure D.2 P(S)A Creation and Update Process; original drawing by colleague
Joost Melsen

(near) environment, whereas a smaller project with say legal focus may have to work with clear business concepts and a focus on preventing non-robust workarounds.

Even so, just an 'it depends' answer to when is a PSA good enough can be quite frustrating to the PSA's author. So we will give a basic checklist of subjects to assess for the quality of a PSA:

3.1 Project dependencies

- Are the project dependencies clear?
- Do you feel you have a complete overview of dependencies?
- Can the project deliver its results in a stable manner with respect to these dependencies? If not, what mitigation options are there via architecture?

3.2 Project result

- In terms of deliverables*, when is the project done?
- In terms of deliverables, what needs to be still done after the project is considered ready? Is there agreement on that?
- Are the deliverables covered by the architecture?
- Has attention been paid to all layers and aspects for all elements? And have all relevant definitions and choices regarding these elements been covered in the architecture?

3.3 Project conditions

Regarding difficult conditions / constraints the project needs to operate under:

---

* Deliverables mean: changes in business, application and infrastructure. Business architecture is mainly meant for determining e.g. completeness and consistency.

- Are there risky or overly ambitious results to achieve from an architectural perspective*? Does the architecture address this risk by approach (e.g. plateaus) or by design (e.g. temporary workarounds)?
- What can you do by means of architecture to relax the project's conditions/constraints?
- Do the conditions/constraints form a risk for the architecture design itself? What would the impact be? How have you mitigated this?

3.4 Project deliverables

- Are you assured of the architectural quality of deliverables that the project is going to deliver? In areas where you are not assured, have you indicated the reasons and implications?
- How long do you think your architecture can be used?
- For areas which cannot yet be defined, are there realistic working assumptions or is there a defined approach to address the area in time?

Towards project end, the following should be in place to have architecture deliverables successfully accepted by the line organization:

- Documentation of deviations from the organization's architecture (FSA and guidelines);
- Specification of the solution (business continuity, information security, IT Service Management characteristics);
- Models that can be added to the Current State Architecture.
- A list of decommissioned Current State Architecture elements

---

Overly ambitious projects are the most likely to fail in keeping to their intended architecture

4   Positioning the PSA in PRINCE2 and in Project Delivery

The diagram on page 210 shows how creating a PSA is positioned with regards to Prince 2 for project management. The concept of having Project Start Architectures and Project Architectures stems originally from Sogeti's Dynamic Architecture method (DYA), which is therefore also included*. In the lower part of the figure, one can also see how the PSA relates to the project execution phase (independent of the project delivery methodology chosen).

4.1   Relations with Prince 2: the project management process

The project executive (normally a manager from a business domain) is accountable for the complete project. This person will instruct the creation of the Project Brief and PID. An essential part op PID is an (EA-reviewed) PSA)

During the startup phase a Project Brief is created. Creating a PSA takes place in the Initiating Project phase. In that phase also a Project Initiation Document (PID) is created. The PSA provides input for the PID[†].

Approving a PID (and actual commencing of project activities) should ideally take place after a positive formal review on the PSA, which is in turn based on content review in the Architecture Board.

The PSA eventually becomes an appendix to the PID. The PID can only be finalized if the PSA has been reviewed. When the PID has been reviewed, the Project Start Architecture can become the Project Architecture. If the PID is delivered without an approved PSA, this must be marked clearly and the review from EA must accompany the PID and the PSA.

---

* However, our version of what a PSA is (as described in this guideline document) differs from what DYA describes, the reason for which is outside the scope of this document.

[†] E.g. for the business case. Without a decent idea of what the project must deliver, the business case is generally based on air.

4.2 Relations with Project Delivery

The PSA content is directive input to the delivery stream(s) of the project. New insights during project delivery may necessitate the project architecture to be updated. The project architect cooperates with analysts/designers/specialists to achieve good alignment between project architecture, designs and actual implementation. In case of changes with substantial impact, it is wise to seek intermediate alignment with Enterprise Architecture. Enterprise Architecture will (minimally) inform or (in cases the AB requires it or if the changes are substantial) consult the Architecture Board.

4.3 References

[1] Link to a published version of the current state model
[2] Link to a published version of the future state architecture
[3] Link to the requirements of the support organization
[4] Link to PSA modeling guidelines (patterns and such)
[5] Link to CSA modeling guidelines (patterns and such)
[6] Link to Business Continuity impact analyses
[7] Link to security classifications and standards
[8] Link to security classifications and standards
[9] Link to operational risk management policies
[10] Link to a risk matrix

Appendix A   Annotated table of contents of a PSA

Note: the table of contents is a guideline. Although adherence to layering and structure will contribute to manageability of the total architecture, the project architect may group subjects in another way for reasons of conciseness, readability or other valid reasons.

210

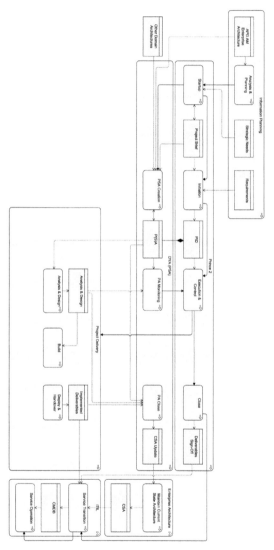

Figure D.3 Relation between PSA and Prince2/Delivery

MANAGEMENT SUMMARY
This chapter contains a concise overview of the most important architectural choices appropriate for a non-architect reader.

1 PROJECT
This chapter contains high level descriptions of the project, who is involved, and the motivation for the project.
1.1 Project context
Introduction to the project, providing the reader with context. Reproduced from mandate, business case or with use of project manager's input.
1.1.1   Project goal
A short description (including main business characteristics of the solution) of the project's goal .
1.1.2   Project organization
Short description of the organization, units and teams involved; names of representatives involved, this is for easy reference to readers who to contact for clarification
1.1.3   Architects involved
List of architects. This concerns of course the project architect. Possibly there are other architects involved. Identify who is (have been) involved for which part of the PSA. This is for easy reference to readers who to contact for clarification
1.1.4   Business benefits
Describe relevant business benefits to achieve in this project, e.g. The business drivers for this project are
- *Drive down maintenance cost (operational excellence)*
- *Implement the Y-model (enhance timeliness of investment positions managed by external managers*

*This is for improving the independent readability of the
PSA, referring to other documents (like a mandate) is
possible but these document should then be included
as background material for the review.*

1.1.5 Timelines / roadmap
When to achieve which result.

1.2 Architecture context

*What are the main architectural drivers (starting points)? What
does this project contribute to e.g. complexity reduction (both
in the short run - because of intermediate transitions - and on
the long term)?. If the project would raise complexity (either
on short or long term), describe here. What does this project
contribute to e.g. flexibility?*

2 BUSINESS AND INFORMATION ARCHITECTURE

This chapter documents the architectural impact of the project in
the area of products and services, processes, and organization, by
defining the architectural design of the target state, and identifying
changes to the current architecture.

2.1 Introduction

If there are concepts or choices that span the business and
information architecture, these can be introduced here.

*Please note: the architect may choose one of the below
perspectives as the dominant one for his table of contents,
and incorporate the other perspectives and views into that. In
practice, grouping is mostly done by business function or by
business process.*

2.2 Actors and roles

This paragraph contains the target state organization after project
execution.

2.2.1 Actor A1

Description (which part of the organization does the change
concern) Change / impact (how does the project impact or
change the actor, is that in/out project scope)

Relevant parameters (e.g. how many individuals/target system users) Design choices (name design choices and identify any deviations from the architecture)

2.2.2 Actor A2
2.2.3 Role R1
2.2.4 ...

⋮

2.3 Products and services

This paragraph defines the design of target products and target services. See under Actors and roles. Products (being aggregates of services and objects) are optional.

2.3.1 Product P1
2.3.2 Service D1
2.3.3 ...

⋮

2.4 Business functions and business processes

This paragraph defines the design of target business functions and target business processes. See under Actors and roles.

2.4.1 Business function BF1
2.4.2 Business process BP1
2.4.3 ...

⋮

2.5 Business Objects

Et cetera.

2.6 Views

Business layer view (total) of the target situation, compliant with our Model Construction Views (at project end; additional/other viewing techniques are possible). General explanations of views, aimed at providing oversight and insight in the entire solution. If necessary, create business layer sub views with specific explanations. E.g.: use colors and/or separate views to identify transition phases.

3   APPLICATION AND DATA ARCHITECTURE

This chapter documents the architectural impact of the project in the area of applications and data, by defining the architectural design of the target state, and identifying changes to the current architecture.

3.1   Introduction

If there are any concepts or choices that span the application and data architecture, these can be introduced here.

Please note: the architect may choose to logically group elements by subject, e.g. by the same grouping as the business architecture, by data flow, or by application platform. Architecture elements as per below are then incorporated in this grouping. To gain oversight, multiple perspectives can be applied in parallel.

3.2   Application services, application functions and application components

This paragraph defines the target application services, application functions and application components. The project architect designs their definitions, and how they are assigned/related.

3.2.1   Application object 1

Composition/decomposition: which services, functions and components belong together. Description (what does the application object do, how does it support the business) Change / impact (how does the project impact or change the current application landscape, is that in/out project scope) Relevant parameters (how many instances, which response times, other parameters) Design choices (name design choices and identify any deviations from our architecture)

3.2.2   ...

:

3.3   Data objects

This paragraph defines the target data objects. A composition may be appropriate. If the project has a strong focus on data processing, it may be useful to include an integral Data-Information

View, to prevent scattered descriptions of the data processing. See under Application services, application functions and application components.

3.3.1 <u>Data object 1</u>

3.3.2 <u>. . .</u>

⋮

3.4 Views

Application layer view (total) of the target situation, compliant with our Model Construction Views. General explanations of views, aimed at providing oversight and insight in the entire solution. If necessary, create application layer sub views with specific explanations. E.g.: use colors and/or separate views to identify transition phases.

4 INFRASTRUCTURE ARCHITECTURE

This chapter documents the architectural impact of the project in the area of infrastructure, by defining the architectural design of the target state, and identifying changes to the current architecture.

4.1 Introduction

If there are concepts or choices that span the infrastructure, these can be introduced here.

Please note: the architect may choose one of the below perspectives as the dominant one for his table of contents, and incorporate the other perspectives and views into that. In practice, grouping is mostly done by node or cluster.

4.2 Infrastructure services

This paragraph defines the target infrastructure services.

List all involved middleware components

List all relevant infrastructural interfaces needed in the project

4.2.1 <u>Infrastructure service 1</u>

Description (what does the infrastructure service do, how does it support the application layer) Change / impact (how does the project impact or change the current infrastructure service / how does the project use the infrastructure service; if the project will make new use of existing services: distinguish between using existing instances and implementing a new (dedicated) instance of the service) Design choices (name design choices and identify any deviations from our architecture)

4.2.2 ...

⋮

4.3 Nodes, system software and devices

This paragraph defines which infrastructural nodes are implemented and configured.

4.2.1 Node 1

Description (which nodes) Change / impact (specify the system software and devices that will make up the nodes) Design choices (name design choices and identify any deviations from our architecture)

4.2.2 ...

⋮

4.4 Network

This paragraph defines which network components are implemented or changed by the project.

4.4.1 Network component 1

Description (which type of network/network path; bandwidth; encryption, ...) Change/impact Design choices (name design choices and identify any deviations from existing architecture choices and guidelines)

4.4.2 ...

⋮

5 Requirements regarding other architectures

5.1 Issues

Unsolved issues with relevance for the project architecture are named here. This paragraph should be empty at project end, or at most contain issues that have been placed outside the project's scope.

5.2 Dependencies

This paragraph contains the (anticipated) design choices that have to be made outside the project and that are prerequisite for the project, even those for which architectural guidelines are absent. Every design choice to be made that the project depends on is described as a requirement.

5.2.1 *Requirement 1 - identifying one-liner*

Requirement

description of the prerequisite for the project

Potential solution(s) (optional)

short high level description of a potential design decision (alternative) in the external architecture, with rationale for the proposed decision

⋮

5.2.N *Requirement N - identifying one-liner*

See under 5.2.1 N.B.1 Requirements of other architectures should be stated in the PID as dependencies, they should be managed by the project manager. If an architectural guideline is absent, the creation of one needs to be coordinated. If a guideline does exist, but the external domain does not comply with it yet, the project dependency is on an activity in the external domain (making the external domain compliant). N.B.2: During the project,new requirements may occur. This Chapter should be updated, the corresponding dependencies should again be managed in the project. N.B.3: If the external requirements cannot be met by the responsible parties (e.g. for additional network requirements of an application), then the project architecture needs to be adapted. A new cycle of architectural and project change will be initiated. As an extreme case, this could lead to stopping the project, in the case that none of the alternatives is acceptable.

*Wisdom is not wisdom when it is derived from
books alone*
Quintus Horatius Flaccus

*Nine-tenths of the existing books are nonsense
and the clever books are the refutation of that
nonsense*
Benjamin Disraeli

E Suggested Reading

THIS LIST is not a complete list of publications that have influenced the contents of this book. Instead, this list is limited to the few resources that have been explicitly referenced in the text; and I have purposely limited referencing, as this book is not a scientific book.

Of this list, these are my suggestions for further reading: Dreyfus, Hacker (or/and Wittgenstein himself), Lewis, Schwarz, Scott-Morgan. And — of course — if you want to go into serious modeling of your enterprise: *Mastering ArchiMate...* (sorry, couldn't resist).

IEE11   (2011). Iso/iec/ieee 42010; systems and software engineering – architecture description. ISO. Online; accessed 20-september-2014.

Bro78   Brooks Jr., F. P. (1978). *The Mythical Man-Month.* 1st edition Addison-Wesley Longman Publishing Co., Inc..

Bro87   Brooks Jr., F. P. (1987). No silver bullet essence and accidents of software engineering. *Computer, 20*(4), 10–19.

Cla96   Clark, A. (1996). *Being There.* MIT Press.

DG08   De Groot, A. D. (2008). *Thought and Choice in Chess.* Amsterdam University Press.

Dij06   Dijksterhuis, A. (2006). On making the right choice: The deliberation-without-attention effect. *Science, 311*, 1005.

Dij69   Dijkstra, E. W. (1969). Structured programming. circulated privately.

Dij72   Dijkstra, E. W. (1972). The humble programmer. Turing Award lecture.

220

Dij77   Dijkstra, E. W. (1977). Zevende toespraak tot mijn stu-
         denten, voorjaar 1977.   circulated privately.

Dre92   Dreyfus, H. L. (1972,1979,1992). *What Computers* Still
         Can't Do. MIT Press.

Hac96   Hacker, P. M. S. (1996). *Wittgenstein's place in twentieth-
         century analytic philosophy*. Blackwell. This is a great
         book on Wittgenstein's role in researching the limits of
         logic and in describing Wittgenstein's unique position as
         three-dimensional philosopher in a world populated by
         flatlanders. Another great source is of course Wittgen-
         stein's own books, especially [Wit94] and [Wit72]..

Lew10   Lewis, B. (2010). Run it as a business – why that's a train
         wreck waiting to happen.   Infoworld, IDG. Online; ac-
         cessed 7-september-2014.

McC04   McConnell, S. (2004). *Code Complete, Second Edition*.
         Microsoft Press.

Sch97   Schwarz, P. (1997). *The Art of the Long View - Planning
         for the Future in an Uncertain World*. 2 edition John Wi-
         ley & Sons.

SM94   Scott-Morgan, P. (1994). *The Unwritten Rules of the
         Game*. McGraw-Hill.

Ses07   Sessions, R. (2007). Comparison of the Top Four Enter-
         prise Architecture Methodologies. Technical Report.

Ses08   Sessions, R. (2008). *Simple Architectures for Complex
         Enterprises*. Microsoft Press.

Wie14   Wierda, G. (2014). *Mastering ArchiMate – Edition II*.
         R&A.

Wit72   Wittgenstein, L. (1972). *The Blue and Brown Books*.
         Blackwell. Wittgenstein changed his views over the
         years. But especially the intermediate Blue Book is very
         accessible (on certain points even more so than [Wit94]).
         The Blue Book contains lectures given by Wittgenstein to
         his students..

Wit84   Wittgenstein, L. (1984). *Tractatus logico-philosophicus [u.a.]*. Suhrkamp.

Wit94   Wittgenstein, L. (1994). *Philosophical Investigations*. Blackwell.

Details count
Peter Weinberger

F Notes

"Program testing can be used to show the presence of bugs, but never to show their absence!"
Edsger Dijkstra — Structured Programming [Dij69]
McConnell: "Testing by itself does not improve software quality. Test results are an indicator of quality, but in and of themselves, they don't improve it. Trying to improve software quality by increasing the amount of testing is like trying to lose weight by weighing yourself more often. What you eat before you step onto the scale determines how much you will weigh, and the software development techniques you use determine how many errors testing will find. If you want to lose weight, don't buy a new scale; change your diet. If you want to improve your software, don't test more; develop better."
Steve C McConnell — Code Complete: A Practical Handbook of Software Construction [McC04]
As an example: before computerized records, a medical researches could maybe do two statistical research projects, as all the data had to be collected by hand from paper origins. When computers were introduced, people expected that — as they could collect the data in minutes instead of months — researchers would be able to spend more time on quality subjects, instead of the boring work of data collection. But what happened was that instead of two research projects, hundreds were done, all adding their own pressure on the

business to handle all that output. Next to higher volumes, the computerization made complex operations possible that were unthinkable in the years before. Complex investment instruments, detailed reporting on customers, citizens, to be regulated businesses became feasible. As a result of all these, formerly unrealistic, possibilities, the world has become far more complex.

[4] We in enterprise architecture and information management often use the same term with different meanings. E.g., the meaning of 'capability' or 'business function' may have a slightly different meaning for people in a discussion, which then leads to truck load of subtle misunderstandings. When we discuss things we tend to assume that the meaning we give a phrase is the same as our discussion partner gives. This is part of what Wittgenstein has labeled the 'bewitchment by language'.

[5] In case you wonder why this statement was on the first page, it is a personal motto and a *leitmotif* of much of my writings. If you read the motto out loud, it says "The world is not rational, it is real".

Forget about the rest of the footnote, unless you are *really* curious, but please remember that the text below is in no way representative for what is discussed in this book. There is no mathematics in the book.

$\mathbb{Q}$ in mathematics is a way to write the set of all *rational* numbers, $\mathbb{R}$ is the sibling symbol that denotes the set of *real* numbers. A rational number is any number that can be written as a quotient of integers, e.g., $\frac{1}{3}$ or $\frac{355}{113}$. There are numbers that cannot be written as quotients of integers, such as $\sqrt{2}$ or π. The set of rational numbers $\mathbb{Q}$ is a subset of the set of real numbers $\mathbb{R}$, the latter is the set of *all* numbers (not quite, but it will do for here). I'm not getting into details (and mathematics does not appear anywhere in the book), but mathematicians have found out that, while there is an infinite amount of integers (you can always go on counting, so infinite but countable, this is called $\aleph_0$), there is a much 'larger' infinite amount of reals (infinite, but uncountable, this is called $\aleph_1$, which is thought to be equal to $2^{\aleph_0}$). By the way, if you think that something like an amount (a number) that is equal to 'two to the power of infinity', or 'two times two times two … ad infinitum', is weird, I won't blame you, but it is the stuff professional mathematics is made of.

Digital computers work in the domain of integers (all the rest, including floating point numbers or reals on a computer, is an elaborate illusion) and not even the infinite version of it. But the real world is not digital at all, it is real. You can grasp this difference by starting with the set of integers. Between every two integers (one, two, three, and so forth) there is an (uncountable) *infinite* amount of numbers, between one and two, and again between two and three, in fact between *any* two different numbers, integer or not, and however close they are together, there is an *uncountable* infinite amount of other numbers ($\aleph_1$). And yes, that means that — weirdly enough — between any two numbers there are as many real numbers as there are real numbers *in total*. Mathematics is weirdly fantastic.

Though it is possible that reality itself is not as infinitely divisible as the mathematical idea of a real number (a question in the domain of fundamental physics), this still illustrates the limitations of the integer numbers with respect to the real world (unless the real world down below is discrete, which I find rather unlikely, but we're in the realm of speculative physics when we are discussing that). And it mirrors some other limitations, such as the limitations of using logic in a real world (Wittgenstein) or the limitation of trying to create human behavior (definitely real, hence a higher order of infinity) with digital computers (definitely finite, so digital 'human intelligence'-type AI is something that will by definition never succeed).

Is that bit of math explanation above any good? Not at all. Is this explanation or the statement important for the book? Also not at all, but I thought I explain it here, in case you are curious about the statement.

6 In 2014, a Dutch newspaper reported about the project's demise, and also noted that the now responsible people had not been able to find the project archive, so a good estimate on how much money had been wasted was not possible.

7 Though I must say this was bungled to an extent I have seldom seen. The architecture was so fundamentally broken it could never have reliably worked and the management of that agency excelled in ignoring or denying problems and acting aggressively against anyone who was critical.

8 Standish originally took three measures: time, budget, and functionality. A project was successful if it was 'under budget', 'on time' and 'delivered all the functionality it set out to do. But as many critics have noted, the best estimate will have a 50% chance of being too high and 50% of being too low. It is therefore to be expected that even with perfect estimates, 12.5% of projects will (over)deliver on functionality and not overshoot on time and budget — in other words: successful projects in Standish' terms are expected to be 12.5% (50% of 50% of 50%) of all projects in the best of cases. In that light, Standish' report that 16%

of projects fell in that category is effectively positive news. There are many other weaknesses in Standish' approach and as a management instrument it is highly unreliable as several critics have shown, but 31% of projects that are cancelled and nothing to show for it remains a sore spot.

[9] These devices will have increasingly rich, and thus complex, interfaces. It is in my opinion very unlikely that we will see real 'intelligent' devices — as human-level intelligence in a digital world is in my view impossible, but that is another story — but we might see some standardization as a reaction on increased complexity. In simple ways, this can already be seen, e.g. the standardization of presentation-interfaces in the current period towards HTML5/CSS3/Javascript.

The whole IoT will also encounter very difficult hurdles. E.g., it is easy to see that a health insurance company will benefit from increasing the health of its customers, as there will be less claims, but ethically, there are large risks to such information — mainly ethical — such as exclusion, which is essentially opposite to the idea of risk-sharing inherent in insurance (and capitalism in general) in the first place. See Immanuel Wallerstein's *The Modern World System* series of books about the history of capitalism, and especially part III on the birth of modern capitalism.

Or economical. Richard Feynman once quipped: "There are 10^{11} stars in the galaxy. That used to be a *huge* number. But it's only a hundred billion. It's less than the national deficit! We used to call them astronomical numbers. Now we should call them economical numbers."

The terms FSA and CSA are not industry standards. I have started to use the acronyms FSA (for Future State Architecture), CSA (for Current State Architecture) and P(S)A for

Project (Start) Architecture. PSA is a term coming from the DYA enterprise architecture framework. In that framework, FSA is called the 'strategic dialogue'. In FEAF, the US government Federal Enterprise Architecture framework, the CSA is the 'baseline' and the FSA is the 'target' architecture.

12 Interestingly, both the ANSI/IEEE standard and its successor, the ISO/IEC/IEEE standard, have a title that makes clear it is about *software system* architecture, not *enterprise* architecture. IEEE Std 1471: "Recommended Practice for Architectural Description of Software-Intensive Systems". ISO/IEC/IEEE 42010: "Systems and software engineering – Architecture description". This does not stop enterprise architectures such as TOGAF to 'embrace' the ISO definition of system architecture and expand the notion of 'a system' to include 'an enterprise'.

ANSI/IEEE Std 1471-2000 was first adopted as ISO/IEC 42010:2007 and later changed into ISO/IEC/IEEE 42010. [IEE11].

13 This has to do with the role that principles and guidelines play in architecture. See page 59 for the two types of role principles may play.

14 The attempt of catching a reality in a large set of rules resembles the attempt of some logical positivists before the second world war to create a footing for philosophy by creating clear definitions. That did not work either. Generally, as Dreyfus already argued forty years ago [Dre92], people working in IT could do worse than spend a little time studying analytic philosophy and learn that some of their attempts have already been tried before in that field, failed there and for the same reasons probably will fail in IT as well.

5 The formal verification movement still exists and Edsger Dijkstra was an important moving force. He wanted to create abstractions that could be proven to be formally correct, which then in turn could be used as elemental elements at higher abstraction levels and so forth, thus proving correctness of a program.

Now, there have indeed been formal correctness proofs of limited sets of logic, including an automated proof of correctness for the division operator in a computer processor (following Intel's blunder in providing a processor with an embedded fundamental mathematical error). But formulating a proof in a world where requirements are perfectly logical might be possible (even if problems of scale exist, the mentioned automatic proof from 1996 is of a very simple binary algorithm of 13 steps; and more recent formal proofs of for instance microkernels have excluded all kinds of aspects, such as self-modification of programs). And such a proof in real-world systems where the requirements touch upon the not strictly logical world of human behavior is yet another matter. Formal proofs require (Dreyfus mentioned a likewise problem when he discussed the 'ontological assumption' behind AI) a complete set of — above all — *discrete* requirements.

Wittgenstein has been credited for the attempt to analyse the use of logic in determining meaning in his *Tractatus*. He summarized this work himself with the statement that if we could not be clear (read: formal) about something, we should keep silent about it, implying: if you cannot be *absolutely* (i.e. formally) certain about the meaning of a statement (e.g. an ethical statement), it could potentially be false and using false statements destroys meaning. What could be gathered under the 'formal meaning' umbrella turned out to be fairly limited. Wittgenstein therefore initially withdraw from philosophy as in his view, nothing more than the precious little he had been able to pin down could be said about it.

But later in life, he approached the same issue from the other side. Given that we are obviously *not* silent about not formalizable issues, our statements must carry meaning after all. The source of that meaning cannot be logical arguments — that was a conclusion of the *Tractatus* — so there must be another source for the fact that statements can have meaning. Analyzing that, he came to the conclusion that (as formulated by P.M.S. Hacker) "meaning lies hidden in correct use".

Dijkstra has been known to like to quote Wittgenstein's statement from the introduction to the *Tractatus*: "what can be said at all can be said clearly, and what we cannot talk about we must pass over in silence." (e.g., in [Dij77], where he makes harsh comments about the social sciences), but the limited practical use of that wisdom that is in Wittgenstein's later thought, never entered Dijkstra's writings (which the comment on the social sciences shows most clearly). Dijkstra was not content that it was in theory possible to prove the correctness of sets of logical statements, such as a computer program on a digital computer, he expanded it to the world of discourse in general. But this logical correctness of computer programs does not equate to meaning, let alone to its meaning in a world that is decidedly *not* formal.

16 Roger Sessions writes in *A Comparison of the Top Four Enterprise-Architecture Methodologies* [Ses07]:

Building a large, complex, enterprise-wide information system without an enterprise architect is like trying to build a city without a city planner. Can you build a city without a city planner? Probably. Would you want to live in such a city? Probably not.

It depends, I would say. Certainly the 'grand design' city parts from just after the second world war are far less popular than the old ones that were 'designed' before city planning was as ubiquitous as it is today. In fact, these days we see city planners and architects returning to the values that came to pass before ambitious city planners took over with grand schemes and architectural principles. For me, all if this sounds pretty familiar. To be fair, Sessions adds:

> Of course, hiring a city planner does not guarantee a livable city; it merely improves your chances. Similarly, having an enterprise architect does not guarantee a successful enterprise architecture. There are many examples of failed enterprise architectures in the world today, and all of them had enterprise architects (probably dozens!).

This probably stems from the fact that the first enterprise architects wanted to draw a distinction between *systems* design and *enterprise* design which should guide the evolution of systems design. They created an *abstraction* of system design instead of seeing it as an *aggregation* of other design. This pattern is reminiscent of Edsger Dijkstra's structured programming; the idea of which was to create logical (mathematical) abstraction on top of logical (mathematical) abstraction *ad infinitum*. Each 'layer' was supposed to be a perfect set of operators to express the next layer in. These perfect abstractions were however hard to create in reality. The industry settled for a much looser, more practical, way: object-orientation (which Dijkstra disliked because it was messy and did not provide a mathematical abstraction).

[18] Even Le Corbusier did not only produce principles and guidelines, but produced actual designs for cities and buildings. The modernists, of which he was one of the most important ones, used a rational, rule-driven architecture principles (e.g. the Athen's Charter for city planning) which led to many urban planning disasters. It is probably also not a coincidence that the rational rule-based approach to urban architecture co-existed with philosophical approaches such as logical positivism. They were all part of a 'Zeitgeist' that believed strongly in the wholesome effect of rational, rule-based, logical approaches to human problems (e.g., Wiener Kreis, logical positivism) which was inspired by Wittgenstein's *Tractatus*. In philosophy, this naïve belief was thoroughly destroyed, mainly by Ludwig Wittgenstein himself, but in the world of IT it has so far kept its foothold, from artificial intelligence to enterprise architecture.

[19] The concept of a relative strength of chess pieces has been given a lot of attention over the last decennia because of its use in computer chess where calculations need to be devised. As a concept it is much older. In the reality of a chess game its use is limited as the strength of a piece may depend on many things, not the least of which is its position on the board. A fully locked-up bishop in a inactive corner of the play is virtually worthless when calculating exchanges. See also Boris Spassky's comment at the start of this chapter.

A tactical rule about valuation may change during the game. Howard Staunton once said:

> The Queen is usually reckoned equal, in average situations, to two Rooks and a Pawn, but towards the end of a game she is hardly so valuable as two Rooks.

Note that, calculated with the earlier mentioned valuation rule, the outcome is quite different. In the other rule, two Rooks and a Pawn equals 11, while the Queen equals 9. This probably has to do with the fact that rooks have limited freedom of movement at the start of the game and only come into their force when the board gets empty.

Dedicated chess supercomputer Deep Blue finally defeated world chess champion Gary Kasparov in 1997, a feat that in the 60's of the previous century by the cognitive scientists and artificial intelligence engineers of the time was predicted to happen within 10 years of time.

Gary Kasparov did not just play the computer, he played against the computer *and* a team of humans (IBM engineers and Joel Benjamin, an international grand master chess who was voted "grandmaster of the year" in 1998) who analyzed the games and between games changed the programming as the computer was unable to learn from its mistakes. Kasparov was at the end tired and lost the last game due to a blunder and with that the match. Kasparov has voiced suspicions that in one of the games the IBM team interfered with the computer, but this has never been proven. IBM dismantled the machine and did not make the logs publicly available. They refused a rematch where Kasparov would have had equal opportunity to analyze the computer.

If Kasparov would not had lost that rematch, he would most likely have lost in the years after, of course, it was a matter of time. But whereas a human like Kasparov evaluates maybe one to two positions per second, Deep Blue in 1997 evaluated 200 million(!) positions per second. Deep Blue calculated six to eight moves ahead and up to twenty in certain circumstances. Kasparov has stated that he generally can think three to five moves ahead and in situations of forced moves as many as twelve to fourteen, but obviously his three to five are not as exhaustive in terms of actual positions evaluated as those from Deep Blue, because it takes a chess master around half a second to evaluate a position completely.

21 A nice example is given in Dreyfus' *What Computers (Still) Can't Do*, in the 1992 edition, where he describes the outcome of a neural network approach that the US Department of Defense used. They used a neural network to train the computer to recognize tanks on aerial photographs. They had a set with identical places, in one set the tank was there, in another it wasn't. They trained the neural network with a part of that set, and afterwards it was able with high precision to recognize tanks in the rest of the set.

Then they gave it new photos from an entirely different set and the neural network program failed miserably. When they analyzed what went wrong, it turned out that the photos in the original set had been prepared specifically for the experiment in advance and both versions, with and without tank, had been taken on different days, without and without cloud cover. What the neural network had learned to recognize, the (hidden) rule it had established, was in fact the availability of sharp shadows or not, representing a clear sky versus cloud cover.

22 There are a few exceptions where simple rules may produce complex or even chaotic results. For instance, the chaotic-looking Mandelbrot sets are produced by very simple rules. Another example is the complex looking spider web, which has been recreated with a couple of simple rules. Such research has fed the belief that complexity is an emerging

property of simple rules, a belief that (see chapter 7) fits cultural prejudices very well.

3 ISO/IEC/IEEE 42010 [IEE11] writes:

> Recent definitions have emphasized architecture as a web of decisions:
>
>> An architecture is the set of significant decisions about the organization of a software system, the selection of the structural elements and their interfaces by which the system is composed, together with their behavior as specified in the collaborations among those elements, the composition of these structural and behavioral elements into progressively larger subsystems, and the architectural style that guides this organization — these elements and their interfaces, their collaborations, and their composition [Kruchten, The Rational Unified Process]
>
> Note the use of *significant* — not all decisions are part of the architecture, but only those that are **fundamental**.

IEEE's change of *significant* into *fundamental* is in fact an important change of focus, inspired by the common conviction in enterprise architecture that enterprise architecture is not about details. The idea that there could be significant *details* is of course known, but quietly ignored as an intractable problem.

The saying is often attributed to Albert Einstein — and it may have been inspired by him, as Harris was told by composer Roger Sessions that he, Sessions, had heard this from Einstein — but it has not been found in Einstein's writings. See http://quoteinvestigator.com/2011/05/13/einstein-simple/

Herbert Simon, the Nobel laureate in psychology heard of the book, ordered it and learned Dutch so he could read it. He saw in it a vindication of his ideas that heuristics were at the basis of human cognition, an idea later to be discredited by Human Dreyfus in his book *What Computers Can't Do* using the same source.

[26] Interestingly, amateurs and grand master were equally able to reproduce nonsense chess board setups, while grand masters were much better at reproducing real positions. This makes it very clear that the grand masters do not photographically remember the basic positions of a chess board setup, but they remember the landscape in terms of more abstract patterns and what they mean. There might be a relation between that and the way some memory-skill boosting techniques use 'additional patterns of meaning' to give the basic thing to remember a meaning beyond the basics, thus employing more of the brain's power.

[27] Protagoras probably needs to be rehabilitated. See the comments at the end of http://masteringarchimate.com/2014/07/08/why-is-stakeholder-not-a-role-in-archimate/

[28] An interesting example is the beliefs behind many 'application rationalization' initiatives. The organization wants to fight the mess of applications by replacing them with off the shelf applications that have arrived on the scene. They count, and what they see is that they can replace tens of applications by a single one. This looks definitely like a simplification of the complex landscape.

But these applications cast such a wide net, that they can better be considered as *platforms*. You can install them, but out of the box they do nothing. You need to *configure* (a weasel term for 'programming', if there ever was one in IT) them to make them do what you need. What then happens is that the functionality in those twenty old applications has to be recreated in the new platform. You end up with twenty *hidden* applications, but with the same complexity as before. The new platform may support building the new applications better, but it also comes with its own 'canned architecture' that may life more difficult here and there.

Recognizing the difference between applications and platforms is very helpful to get a grip on the real complexity of both current state and target state. Here, modeling with a decent enterprise architecture modeling language such as ArchiMate with decent modeling patterns and standards [Wie14] is useful in preventing self-deception.

[9] 'Visibly' means: they spend substantial time on it themselves. If they only regularly state how important it is, but they do not spend time on it, they are not actually thinking it is important at all. It is not what people *say*, it is what they *do* that is important (see also *The Unwritten Rules of the Game* [SM94]). And if you are a manager reading this: if you think it is important, ask help from your enterprise architects in getting management involved and up to speed. Unless you do that, the enterprise architecture results you desire will not come to pass.

And neither does using a separate 'security architecture framework'. Security is an integral part of architecture, the idea of a separate 'security architecture' (such as SABSA) makes no sense and only leads to a 'governance hell'.

The following three, I think, are the most important: being analytic, able to learn quickly and charm.

Even here, there are sometimes sensible discussions. For instance, having DTAP environments for all your applications may be very costly. It more or less multiplies your infrastructure by a factor of four from what is needed for Production. So, sometimes, smart choices can be made. For instance, suppose your Production environment needs a fallback environment in a different data center for continuity reasons. Suppose this is not a 'hot' fallback (immediately takes over) but a 'cold' fallback; when the main production environment goes down, the second must be brought up within a day. You could save money by using that fallback system for other tasks when it is not needed, instead of it sitting idle. You could for instance, use it as Test or Acceptance. That means that when it is needed, the Test or Acceptance setup must be shut down and saved, and the copy Production environment must be brought up. Continuity for Test or Acceptance is not guaranteed, but for Production it is. This is not the same as using a Test or Acceptance environment in Production, it is in fact quickly switching infrastructure from a Test or Acceptance role to a Production role. But in most cases this will be seen as breaking the separation rule between DTAP environments.

[33] This assessment of outsourcing is related to the 'agile' movement for software development.

The current project management and IT project breakdown structures (business analysis, functional designs, technical designs, build, test) were created when we were actually building very simple systems with very clear uses such as the early accounting systems. But the complex requirements of today, e.g., think of all the difficult requirements surrounding patient records, which include variable and fuzzy ethical issues, conflicting societal pressures and so forth, cannot be handled that way, they need more variable methods. This is true for enterprise architecture as it is for software engineering.

34 Microsoft, Nokia and RIM have spectacularly failed at handling disruptive innovations. Especially Microsoft — with almost unlimited financial resources — has failed to answer user experience innovations (personal audio, smartphone, tablets) from Apple, search and advertising innovations from Google, social network innovations from Facebook and Twitter, and has produced a long series of flops. But the innovators themselves are also not always successful, e.g. Apple in social networks, Google in social networks or smartphones (where they freely support a large platform, Android, but are not making money from it (in fact, they spectacularly lost money on it by buying and selling Motorola Mobility) and the only one so far making serious money from Android seems to be Samsung, which is not so much an innovator, but makes money by mainly copying Apple, and is now (2014) in the process of being squeezed by Chinese manufacturers such as Huawei and Lenovo).

35 There are situations where such an approach may work. In situations where there is little uncertainty about what is needed in a few years time, in situations where these *requirements* are actually robust under the uncertainties. This may be when the uncertainty is low (e.g. responding to developments in demographics). And it may be the case when the requirements themselves are robust under uncertainties. An example might be that for a chip machine producer, the actual use of their machines may be uncertain (where will the growth be? mobile? desktop?), but a given is that the size of transistors must come down to lower power per performance.

At this point it is important to note that when I use the term logic, I mean the discrete kind, the kind working with the values true and false, the kind of logic generally employed by analytical philosophy, such as in Wittgenstein's *Tractatus Logico-Philosophicus* [Wit84]. There are many kinds of logic, quantum logic, matrix logic, modal logic, et cetera. Some of these might not have the effect that 'classical' logical rules have, but those are not the ones playing that role in our culture. Much more can be said about this, but this is not the place.

[37] A fate that can easily happen to this book as well. It's neither a popular, nor a culturally acceptable message.

[38] It is to be expected that cloud providers will become 'richer' in terms of the integration features they offer. This will help in managing problems with integrating multiple cloud-silos, but this also means that cloud-silos become just so many more building blocks for the organization, together forming a new level of complexity. Maybe we should at that point invent *enterprise and environment architecture (EAEA)* to be used as term instead of just 'enterprise architecture'.

243

Any inaccuracies in this index may be explained by the fact that it has been sorted with the help of a computer
Donald Knuth — Sorting and Searching

G   Index